PLAY BIG

PLAY BIG

Dr. Jen Welter

with Stephanie Krikorian

SEAL PRESS

Seal Press
Hachette Book Group
1290 Avenue of the Americas, New York, NY 10104
sealpress.com
@SealPress

Printed in the United States of America

Published by Seal Press, an imprint of Perseus Books, LLC, a subsidiary of Hachette Book Group, Inc.

The Hachette Speakers Bureau provides a wide range of authors for speaking events. To find out more, go to www.hachettespeakersbureau.com or call (866) 376-6591.

The publisher is not responsible for websites (or their content) that are not owned by the publisher.

Print book interior design by Jeff Williams

Library of Congress Cataloging-in-Publication Data has been applied for.

ISBN: 978-1-58005-683-0 (hardcover)
ISBN: 978-1-58005-684-7 (e-book)

LSC-C

10 9 8 7 6 5 4 3 2 1

To my football family—men and women,
all the girls and women in the game, and
everyone out there with just a dollar in your
pocket but gold in your heart. Play big.

Contents

Defining Moments

1977   Jennifer Welter is born to Dr. Peter and Nancy Welter and her older sister, Rachel, in Vero Beach, Florida.

1982   Mesmerized by her town's Friday night football enthusiasm, Welter thinks football players are larger-than-life gladiators.

1983   Welter visits her cousins and begs them to pull the mattress out onto the back porch. She runs into them and spends hours getting tackled onto that mattress.

1984   Welter ditches the princess Halloween costume she left her house wearing and dresses up like a football player at a friend's house, foreshadowing an unimaginable destiny.

1985   Welter takes up tennis, spending hours on the court. She falls in love with the sport and eventually travels around the state to compete in tournaments.

1991   Welter's dreams of becoming a professional tennis player are shattered when a coach tells her that she is too small to make it in the sport. She takes up team sports instead.

1996   Welter must decide between Boston College for business or soccer at Claremont McKenna. She sees a prophet to help her decide but ignores the prophet's wisdom.

1996   Welter discovers rugby at BC and plays all four years. Between junior and senior year, she is recruited to try out for the under-twenty-three national team. At just five-foot-two and 130 pounds, she is promptly told, once again, she is too small.

2000   After graduation, she gets a job as a headhunter in downtown Boston. To maintain her sanity, she plays in a flag football league on weekends, which tees up her future in football.

2001   Welter quits her job, gives up her swanky apartment, spends a month back at her old high school in preparation for her tryout for the Mass Mutiny, a team in the National Women's Football League (NWFL). She makes the team.

2004   After two seasons, Welter leaves the Mutiny and moves to Dallas with her fiancé. She plays for the Dallas Dragons in the spring season and plays for the Dallas Diamonds in the fall league.

2004   The Diamonds win the championship, the first of four. A women's football dynasty is born.

2005   Welter receives her first-ever paycheck for playing professional football: $12, $1 per game for the 2004 season with the Diamonds. She saves the check as a reminder that dreams do come true.

2005   Welter completes a master's degree in sport psychology and begins working toward her PhD in psychology.

2008 Welter walks away from the house she owns and lives out of her car for several months. Unable to afford health insurance, which the league requires players to carry, her ability to play football is jeopardized, but she finds creative ways to remain on the team.

2010 Welter helps Team USA win gold at the International Federation of American Football Women's World Championships. Each player must pay $3,000 to represent her country.

2013 Welter and Team USA again win gold. Her dissertation is published and she earns her doctorate.

2014 Welter makes history as the first female to play running back in men's professional indoor football with the Texas Revolution.

2015 Welter becomes the Texas Revolution's linebacker and special teams coach, making history once again breaking another huge barrier.

2015 In July, the Arizona Cardinals hire Welter as the assistant inside linebacker coach to Larry Foote for training camp and preseason, making her the first woman in history to coach in the NFL.

2016 Welter travels the nation as an ambassador for women and girls in sport, representing how to stay true to a dream. She speaks on panels about income inequality; stumps for Hillary Clinton; participates in the White House's United State of Women campaign with the likes of Meryl Streep, Tina Fey, Oprah Winfrey, and other luminaries; and joins Like a Girl and other campaigns.

2016   Welter launches the A Day in the Life of an NFL Player program that teaches women how to play football and provides football players access to coaching opportunities.

2017   Welter is named head coach of Australia's inaugural women's national football team.

When there's no road map in life, you make your own.

||||||||||||||||||||||||||||||||||||||||||||||||||||||||||||||||||||||||||||||||||||||||||||

The Noteworthy Coach

When I started playing football, I knew I was stepping into my destiny. What I didn't know was exactly what that would mean. I just promised myself I would rise to every challenge the game presented, but I never imagined how big those challenges would be or how far I would go. On a journey like mine, there were no road maps or paths to follow because no one else had been there before. I kept playing, trusting that my destiny was in front of me. I knew there was something bigger for me—I just had no idea what it was.

THE NIGHT BEFORE my historic first game as a coach in the NFL, I wanted to do something special for my players. I'd been hired by Arizona Cardinals head coach Bruce Arians as an assistant coach to work with the team's inside linebackers during training camp and the preseason. It was an enormous opportunity—momentous. I was breaking the "glass sideline," the first female coach. The NFL no longer stood for the *No Female League*. This was a significant moment in the history of football, forever changing the league.

I'd made history twice before in men's professional football. First, with the Texas Revolution in the men's Indoor Football League. I was the first woman to step onto the field to play running back against men. Then, the following season, the team hired me to coach—another first.

However, as big as those moments were, I never dreamed the NFL was a possibility, and yet, here I was. The Arizona Cardinals were hosting the Kansas City Chiefs, and I would be on the sidelines as a member of the coaching staff.

I secluded myself in my hotel room to avoid the questions and commentary surrounding the upcoming game. The phrase *you could cut the tension with a knife* came to mind. It felt as though everyone was holding their collective breath, waiting to see what would happen when, for the first time, a woman appeared on the sidelines of an NFL game as a coach. Would the institution of football collapse? Would players forget how to play? Would the game be irreparably harmed and lose its inherent toughness? The hype was too much for me. I escaped the noise, but my mind was far from quiet.

Though this night was clearly different, this feeling was not. I thought about when I was a player, in pregame moments in the locker room, when I was alone in my head, alone with my mind, sometimes a little self-doubt or nerves or emotions crept in. As I contemplated my pregame moments, my mind went to my players. They would have their own pregame moments, their own inner monologue prior to tomorrow's kickoff. For some, this was it, that first NFL game—the culmination of a lifelong pursuit for those guys who touched a football for the first time as young boys, fell in love with the game, and chased down the dream of playing professional football. They were about to make that dream come true. Every player had his own battle that escalated with each game, they were all playing for their future with the team, and, in different ways, each player had to define himself, redefine himself, establish himself, and prove himself. Training camp was one thing, but game day is a completely different animal. As I thought about each individual linebacker, I wished I could have just a few moments with each player to revisit key points we had discussed in practice, but it was too late for that.

Wrestling with anticipation of the biggest moment of my life, I realized: I couldn't be with my players in the locker room, but my words could be. I would write each of my linebackers a note. As a player, that's what I would have wanted from my coach, and I could be the coach that I would have wanted.

I had just enough time to sneak out of the training camp bubble. I stepped into that hot August night and grabbed a Lyft to a shopping center.

It had been a long time since I was in a Hallmark store. I wanted simple notecards, yet as I explored the aisles, it was so overwhelmingly bright, floral, and glittery that I questioned my decision to buy cards. It was sensory overload, and I was realizing that I may have lost all my senses. What was I even thinking coming here? Oh, yeah, great idea, Coach. Was I temporarily insane? Had training camp caused me to lose my mind? Quite possibly.

The exit was close, but one step before crossing back into the mall, a scene from my last Texas Revolution practice before I left for training camp with the Cardinals flashed in my mind. I recalled powerful words from former NFL player Terry Glenn: "The best advice I can give you about coaching in the NFL is to be 100 percent authentic. If you are exactly the same person you were with us every day in practice, those guys will absolutely love you. However, if you are fake in any way, they will sense it, and they will eat you alive."

Damn, backing out was not an option. This was the right thing. This was authentic. Hallmark was not about to intimidate me. I turned around.

Hidden in the wedding section, so not immediately catching my attention, I found plain white cards with an embossed heart on the front—crazy enough to be just right. Heartbeat, right in the center of the defense, involved in the run game and the pass game. Linebackers are the heartbeat of the defense. We set the tone; our impact, pace, and emotions affect the entire defense. We play hard, everyone plays hard. The impact and energy are palpable, contagious.

In 2013, when I'd played on Team USA in the International Federation of American Football (IFAF) Women's World Championship, we thumped our hearts twice with our fists to symbolize that we, the linebackers, were the heartbeat of the defense. I brought that idea with me to the NFL. The cards were perfect.

Back at the hotel, I feverishly wrote notes. I blocked out all distractions with music, and the words just flowed. I stayed up almost all night, in fact, personalizing each note so that it would hit home and resonate with each player. I instructed one under-sized guy to *play big*, that he *didn't have to be big to play big*. At five feet, two inches, I lived that sentiment myself. I told another player to *be as contagious on the field as his personality was off the field*. I encouraged another to be the leader I knew he was *in every single play*. To one of my faster yet lighter guys: *Use your speed and leverage; you don't have to out-big them*. To my huddle caller: *Own your position; leave no doubt, every time you step on the field, with every huddle you command and with every call you make*. Each note was different because each player was different, and what made each player different was what made him great. The unifying word for all my linebackers: *#heartbeat*.

The next morning, as I got ready to go to the game, it dawned on me: although I knew where the stadium was and had been there for practice, I had never really *been* there—not like I was going to be there today. I had never before checked in to the University of Phoenix Stadium *as a coach for an* NFL *game.*

I gathered the notecards in the mandatory clear bag and headed to the stadium. It was surreal. I probably would have been overwhelmed by the bigness of the moment had I stopped to think about it. There had been so much chatter about how it was going to play out—to have a female coach in the NFL. Would it work? Was it doable? It was huge, but focusing on my players had saved me from the voice of doubt; hopefully, the notes would do the same for my players when they found them in their lockers. Those cards were my best way of expressing my empathy. I knew what my linebackers were going through; this was their dream, too.

Before entering the stadium, I ducked into the coachs' office to see our defensive coordinator, James Bettcher.

"Hey, Bettch, I have a question."

He spun around and looked at me. "What's up, Coach?"

"Well," I said, "I have some notes for the guys for the game. Is it okay if I have them put in their lockers?"

"Oh, Coach, no," he said, shaking his head. "We already have the game plan installed. It's a little late for notes."

He was thinking of very different notes from the ones I had in hand. Which made me ever so briefly question what I had done.

"Oh, Bettch," I said, "not that kind of note. These are notes of encouragement, like mental reminders for the guys on playing fast, and leadership . . . those kinds of things."

He paused, and I clutched my clear bag closer to my chest. It became painfully obvious that nobody in the NFL had ever gone to a Hallmark store, bought notecards with hearts on them, and put them in the football players' lockers, much less the 250-pound linebackers' lockers. Anticipation of his response overwhelmed me, and in that ten-second pause I questioned whether there was a place for handwritten cards—and the person who wrote them—in the NFL. But then I choked down my sliver of self-doubt and stood firmly confident that I'd done the right thing.

He broke the silence with, "Oh . . . that's a really good idea. Great thinking, Coach. Absolutely, just give them to the equipment guys. Tell them I said it was OK. They'll put them in."

I let out a silent sigh of relief. Little did I know then that not only was there a place in the National Football League for those notecards and the person who wrote them but also that the impact of those cards would be so dramatic.

A Moment in History

Later, while the guys were in the locker room, a significant pregame moment was taking place in the stadium. Wearing my white Cardinals shirt, I stepped onto the field for a sideline-shattering meeting—a moment that's been enshrined in the Pro Football Hall of Fame: Sarah Thomas, the first full-time female referee in NFL history, and I, the first female coach in NFL history, shook hands and exchanged a few words.

Earlier, when my linebackers found out she was going to referee our game, they joked about how epic it would be if I got in her face and challenged a call. I commented that if things got heated over a call she made, I could handle it; I was, after all, a linebacker. We had all laughed about it.

So, when Sarah and I had our pregame moment, we smiled as we spoke. Afterward, everybody wanted to know what we had talked about that made us laugh as we stood under the lights in front of the crowd. I love that knowing what we said to each other kept everybody else guessing. I'll tell you what it was: I shared with Sarah that we had been the topic of conversation at practice and that of course the linebackers thought it would be good for the cameras if we threw down over a play. Her reaction was priceless. She said she'd seen my game film and wanted no part of being taken out by this particular linebacker.

A handshake between coach and referee, an every-game occurrence that had happened countless times over the history of the game, so normal, and yet, this particular handshake created a new normal on the sidelines that day. Until that moment, women couldn't envision themselves in the game, as a referee or as a coach, much less in the Pro Football Hall of Fame. Before then, it wasn't an option or even a dream for women, not in the roughest, toughest sport in the United States. Until that moment, women might only see themselves on the sidelines—as a reporter, a cheerleader, or a trainer.

But then, Sarah and I shook hands in the spotlight. We had penetrated deep into what had until then been a man's world. If that can happen, well then, it's fair to say women can do just about anything.

My Football Legacy

My story is not just a football story. It's a life story that happened to take place on the football field. By sharing some of my experiences I want to teach you how a five-foot-two female grew to find her place in the most unlikely of sports, one that has been referred to as the final frontier for women in sports. This story is about defying the odds and overcoming them. I did this by adhering to a personal philosophy I call *Play Big*. What I lack in height, I find in stature.

As individuals, each one of us encompasses a unique set of skills, experiences, talents, strengths, fears, limitations. Who you are and what you bring is special. Play Big is about the size of your impact, not the size of your physical being. On a team, to Play Big means to have an impact that is bigger than the individual plays you make, but the philosophy is more than strictly for teams. To Play Big is to emphasize your contribution to the collective—whether that's your school, your company, your community, the world at large—to be acutely aware of the effect your presence has on everyone around you. Do you challenge people to dig deeper, go harder, be better, run faster? On a team, can you play up to the expectations of your coaches and teammates while inspiring them to play big, too? You can do the same as a leader in life—help others to play into their bigness.

I was so proud to be making progress for women with Sarah and at the same time to show caring for the guys with my notecards. Though I hadn't mentioned to anyone other than Bettch that I had written the cards, one of my linebackers was so moved by my words and the gesture itself that he told the press how much the card meant to him. I was surprised later when a reporter asked me on camera about the notes and whether I wrote them because I hold a degree in psychology or because I'm a woman. The answer: neither, really. Those notes were something I would have wanted as a player. A message like that written for me on game day. Was it a slightly girly move? I guess some people might call it that, but I would rather say it was a smart move.

Yes, I brought a unique perspective—as a woman, as a coach, as a former player—to the sport. But empathy, the ability to play a game in someone else's cleats, is neither a uniquely female nor male trait; it is a leadership trait. Period.

For the most part, what I wrote in the cards was never publicized, but my act of giving them came to define me. From that point on, I wrote cards for every single game. And for the last game I coached, I added a twist (which I'll tell you about later) to motivate those million-dollar players. I never imagined that little things, like leaving notes in lockers and teaching these guys what it meant to *Play Priceless,* would influence the game, but they did.

Eventually, they came to call me the "noteworthy coach." My card writing became national news, mostly because one player, Kevin Minter, vocalized how he'd never had a coach show they cared before in that way. When I chastised Kev about sharing the notes with the press, he simply said, "Coach, that was special. They needed to know."

Immune to the Word *No*

As you read this book, I hope you're inspired. Here, I've written note cards for you, too, as guidance and encouragement. You're opening your metaphoric locker as you turn these pages—I've written these cards for you, just like I did for my guys on the team, and my notes frame each chapter.

I share stories that I hope resonate with you. I wove them together in these pages to give you strength on your own journey. I want you to follow your heart, find a dream, and see it out as far as it will possibly take you. Even if you're not playing football, don't worry—motivation is universal. It transcends sport. I want to motivate you. I want you to know that you can accomplish anything with hard work and perseverance.

Think of me as your coach. I'm encouraging you to play big. I've taken hits on and off the field and broken barrier after barrier after barrier—a living testament to the fact that it can be done. I want you to do the same. There's simply no stopping you. My hope is that by the end of this book, you'll be inspired to dream the unimaginable. You'll be unstuck from whatever is holding you back from getting out there and changing the world, your world or the world of someone you know and care about. From doing something you never thought doable. From blazing a trail not yet taken. I followed my dream without having a role model; there was no path to follow, no inkling that making it to the biggest stage in sport could happen for a woman. My point: you never know what's out there to go for until it's out there to go for. Remember that, too. In my gridiron journey, there was no certainty, only hope and a belief in something bigger. There was no way to envision myself in any of the places that I ultimately busted through because, as a woman, it was unimaginable.

To all of that, I'm sure you can relate. Maybe not in sports but certainly in life.

Throughout my journey, I promised myself that despite the hardships, the hurdles, the *Do Not Enter* signs, and the lack of a guiding beacon, I would follow my football dream as far as it would go. I hope that I cleared a path and can act as a guide and a beacon for future generations of women to do the same. Let your dream take you as far as it will; step into your destiny.

You do not have to be big to play big. I did not always realize that. It took me many hits on and off the football field to find the strength to get back up after a knockdown. I had to seek out people and reasons that motivated me to play bigger than I could on my own. I had to shift my perception and own my outlook to help me play big and create the reality of my dreams. I had to realize that everything that made me wrong could actually make me right. As a person who was too small, too old, too short, and too female, I would make history in men's professional football three times by being bold enough to grab life by the balls and step into my destiny, by refusing to play the game by their rules, and by being 100 percent authentic. And now I'm going to show you how to do the same: to dream big and find that unimaginable field on which to stand and live your passion. You might not see it immediately, but it is out there.

I knew football was my destiny, but I never envisioned just how far this game could take me. I worked to be strong and certain in my strengths and at the same time humble and honest about my weaknesses. When I started playing, the biggest accomplishment that could be achieved by a woman was winning the women's equivalent of a Super Bowl. Sometimes, I think God put blinders on me in my life to protect me, to help me keep my head down in the work and my feet on the path, because if I had seen the heights possible, I might have been blinded by the stadium lights.

|||||||||||||||||||||||||||||||||||||||||||||||||||||||||||||||||||||||||||

1

Play Your Own Game

Greatness is not an accident. Greatness is a choice you make over and over and over. And when you choose personal greatness—big or small—it becomes a part of who you are. Don't get me wrong: just like you, I have had days when I would not have chosen greatness on my own. It took work. It took strategy. It took perseverance. Don't leave your greatness to chance.

TAPPING INTO YOUR potential, your ability to play big, requires digging deep, learning as much as you can about yourself, shifting your outlook, and never letting a *no* get you down. For me, finding the game I was meant to play and understanding how to step into my potential took years and many false starts and setbacks.

If only I knew as a kid what I know now.

When I was young, my sister Rachel and I both did after-school activities, tennis and horseback riding among them. One year come sign-up time, my mom suggested we specialize in one sport. It made sense to focus and really kick butt at one thing. I was fiercely competitive in everything I did, in part because I was fearless, as many kids are. But still, I didn't want to compete with my older sister. She was so good with horses, so I decided, *I'll be really good at something else. I'll make tennis my sport. I can be the best at tennis.*

Once I decided on tennis, my parents signed me up for instruction at a nearby club. I took lessons year-round from the time I was eight years old. I was hooked—I loved the sport. I got so into playing tennis, I was on the court for hours every day. It lifted me up in every area of life. It made me feel strong and powerful, like I could do anything.

Once I started playing, I also started watching tennis on TV. It was the one place where female athletes could be visible, could excel. At that time, no other women's sports were broadcast with any regularity. I loved watching Steffi Graf and Gabriela Sabatini and Zina Garrison, and the more I got into the sport, the more I learned about star players such as Chris Evert and Billie Jean King and Martina Navratilova. I saw them and wanted to be them. Here were these athletes—women—and they were strong and talented and beautiful. They were gorgeous in their element: excellence in motion. That power captivated me. I wanted to embody their power. I was enchanted. I thought, *That's what a woman should be.*

My aunt Jackie took me to watch my first professional sporting event, the Virginia Slims of Los Angeles tennis tournament. Watching those matches was surreal. I was so close to these superhero goddesses and all of their greatness. I got everyone's autograph on my racket cover, thinking that would give me their power. I wanted to be among them.

At home, on my court, I was somewhat alone in my ambition. Adults played, but few young girls hit the court like I did; maybe there were two others in my city. So, I challenged myself to play the boys. After all, what would those wonderful, powerful women who inspired me do? Take on the boys and beat them, of course!

One summer, when I was ten years old, the tennis club where I played posted a notice: whoever played the most tennis over a thirty-day period would be awarded a $100 gift certificate. As soon as I learned about that contest, I decided I was going to win it. No question, no hesitation, I was going to do everything in my power to win that gift certificate. I hit it hard. I played every single day. I dragged anybody and everybody who would play tennis with me out onto those courts. I was undeterred.

Of course I won that $100. I felt ten feet tall. I beamed with pride. I used the money at the club shop to buy shirts that had alligators playing tennis on them. I thought they were awesome, so I bought three. I wore them all the time and I thought I was supercool.

How I entered that contest with such determination definitely provides insight into my personality, but the challenge also represented a turning point in my tennis game. I played so much, with so many different people, that I got really, really good.

Keep in mind, I was a tiny, scrawny kid. At the time not even five feet tall, I had this relentless heart. Despite my size, I would fight it out on the court, and that heart kept me winning and kept me in matches. I had the competitive edge and perseverance an athlete needs to go all the way. Even when I played bigger girls, who had shot up and who towered over me—it felt like they were six feet tall, and they might as well have been—it didn't matter. I had the right attitude: I thought big. I was, in my mind, unstoppable. Just before one match at the girls' state team tennis tournament, one very tall girl said, "I hate to break it to you, little girl, but I think I'm going to crush you." I beat her 8 to 3. As I left the court, I said, "I hate to break it to you, but I think I just crushed you." That was my attitude. I didn't talk smack until I beat you.

There were stronger and bigger girls, but none were more tenacious than I was.

I played both singles and doubles and traveled all over the state for tournaments. I was ranked as a singles player in the state of Florida. Around that time I decided I wanted to be a professional tennis player, like all the big-name women I'd watched on TV playing in Wimbledon and the US Open. I was certain I'd found my calling—that one thing I was both passionate about and excelled at.

After doing some research, my parents made arrangements for us to meet with a man who was supposed to be one of the best coaches in the area. He could up my game and help me get to where I wanted to be in the sport.

When we went to meet the coach, I was certain he would see in me what I saw in myself: a winner. A competitor. A girl with a future in tennis. But all he saw was my size. The problem was he couldn't see my heart. He couldn't read my attitude. And, though nobody could defeat me with their size, he defeated me with his words: "Due to your size and your build, you'll never be strong enough to play pro tennis. You're wasting your time." That's all that I remember from that conversation.

I didn't throw my racket down or have a fit or even cry. I didn't leave that day thinking, *He's right. It's over for me.* In fact, I didn't quit tennis that day—not physically anyway. In my heart, though, I think I did. That love for the sport, it faded like a slow leak in a tire. I played here and there, but I found other things to do with my time. I kept hearing his words and thinking if I was wasting my time, *why bother?* Even beating the older kids and the bigger kids, which I had loved to do, wasn't enough to pull me through the harsh reality of his words, the impact of his *no*. That meeting eventually crushed me. Tennis, it seemed, was no longer my destiny.

After hearing that I'd never get to where I wanted to be—I'd never go pro—I started to question why I was doing any of it. Why was I working so hard to get court time? Why was I playing with all my heart for no good reason? It was the first time in my life someone had completely placed a limit on my dreams. For the first time, doubt crept into my young psyche. Maybe I wasn't as good as I thought I was. Where I used to see open skies, I started to see ceilings.

COACH JEN: CEILING BUSTERS

Many girls start to doubt themselves around the time they become teens. They stop showing confidence. They stop showing a desire to win. They don't want to make other people feel bad, and they want to be liked. This shift carries over later in our lives. We can't revert back to fearlessness until we understand what initially made us feel small. Do you have a "tennis moment" in your life? Can you remember a ceiling being placed above you? Think about right now: Is there a ceiling on your dream?

Try to see beyond that ceiling. What would happen if you smashed through it? What's the path to cracking through? You don't need to see the full path at this exact moment, but you do need to figure out what put the ceiling there in the first place and see beyond that.

Nobody Can See What's in Your Heart

The problem with that tennis coach's snap judgment was twofold: His ability to see only the very end of my quest—becoming pro, rather than the journey and all that I might have achieved along the way—was terribly short-sighted. Second: I listened to him. The truth is this: *heart is the one thing that can never be quantified and can never be counted out.* Heart is an important part of any equation that we must remember to factor in when striving for a dream or assessing ourselves.

Let's break that down a little bit.

Problem 1: Heart can't be quantified. Nobody can judge your full potential because, in reality, they don't know the size of your heart. So you have to show them. Give them examples not only of what you've achieved but also the struggles and hurdles you overcame to get there. Don't be afraid to reveal the unpolished side of the journey, not just the end result. That shows heart. Demonstrate what you've learned along your journey, not just in your brain but in your heart as well. You'll find that once you open up, people will relate. And if you're assessing a person, look for heart. Use that as a measure of someone's overall skill set.

Problem 2: We concede to the judgment of others far too often. Don't listen to anybody who tells you *no*. To get past a no, you need to know what is in your heart and *you* need to trust it. I was just too young to trust it with tennis. I didn't have enough life experience to feel determined to prove that coach wrong, to ask someone else for an opinion, to ignore the naysayers. As an adult I do.

In fact, if I were able to speak to my younger self today, I would say, "If you work as hard as you do every day and you continue to play that hard, there's no sport you can't play. There's nothing you can't do." That's recognizing heart. And to anyone struggling with someone else's negativity, I say, don't ever let anybody take away your dreams by putting a ceiling above you because of their own ignorance and insecurity.

I have no doubt that I could have played college tennis. That alone would have been a win for me. But that coach, he didn't realize the damage he did. He stole those dreams from me, and I let him. He put limits—a ceiling—on me. But, hey, maybe he was right. Maybe I wasn't strong enough to play pro tennis.

So, I grew up to play pro football instead.

Give Others around You the Tools to Accomplish Anything

If you're in a position of power or leadership, meaning you're the one doing the assessing, don't say no too quickly. We tell kids to respect authority. But we also need to arm them with the knowledge that nobody but them knows their full potential and that just because one person doesn't see it doesn't mean it's not possible. If another adult back then had known what I was struggling with, I think that person might have corrected my thinking.

There's simply no reason to tell people what they can't accomplish. Why not give them the best tools and let the dream take them as far as it takes them? Before you say no,

- Think about the short-term benefits of your mentees' dreams and encourage them to tackle those dreams. If someone wants to be an actress, for example, maybe she won't win an Oscar. But community theater might give her an outlet to satisfy her dream.

- Help them identify realistic steps that might get them to their big finish, while helping them understand the landscape of their industry.

- Always let them dream big.

Refine Your Message When the Answer Is No

When it's absolutely necessary, there's also a better way to tell somebody no; refine your message and find a way to make it positive. I learned this in high school from the boys' football coach. Like the tennis coach, he told me no once, but the football coach did it in a way that allowed me to see my strength, not dwell on my weakness. I was one of the superstars on the girls' soccer team. I was a sweeper, and I had a reputation for taking everyone out. I was protective of my people. You were not going to get to my keeper through me. I wore number 13 because I was bad luck for the other team. The referees all knew me. They would come up to me before games and be like, "Number 13, we're watching you today."

I loved soccer, but not as much as I loved football. I wanted to test myself on the football field. I'd watch the guys play and think, *I'm as good as they are.* One day, I gathered up my courage and approached the coach.

"Coach Bethel," I said, "you should just let me play football."

"You know what, Miss Welter?" he said. "You are a heck of an athlete. You probably could help my football team, but I'm going to ask you not to play, and let me tell you why."

Before he could finish his sentence, anger washed over my entire body. My head was spinning and I struggled to think of a comeback. Though I had expected him to say "girls can't play football" or something horrible like that (and, if he had, I would have proved him wrong), his answer surprised me.

"I'm a football guy," he continued. "Been one my whole life. And we football guys are the worst kind. Let me tell you what would happen if you played football. Miss Welter, you would go out there, and you're an athlete, so you would make some guy look bad. And he would cheap shot you. I would kill him and go to jail. Miss Welter, please don't play football."

Though his answer was no, it was not a vote of no confidence. It was a show of respect, so I respected his request and didn't play. Years later, I trained with Coach Bethel and his football team to prepare for my tryout with the Mass Mutiny in the National Women's Football League. His coaching helped me get selected for my first football team. And Coach Bethel, to this day, tells everyone his first player to go pro was a girl.

COACH JEN:
MAKE A *NO* INSPIRATION TO LAND A *YES*

- *Take NO as a challenge.* Turn it into *NOw* instead by adding a little *w,* as in *win: NOw* what are you going to do to turn your *NO* into a *win*?

- *Arm yourself.* You have to trust yourself as a dreamer. By trusting your gut and allowing yourself to dream, you are in fact arming yourself to succeed.

- *Let no inspire you.* If you're passed over for a promotion or an opportunity, if you don't achieve something you want to achieve on the first try, you need to muster up the courage and adjust your mentality so that hearing what you couldn't and shouldn't and wouldn't do inspires you to do it anyway.

There's Always Time to Learn a Lesson

Sometimes we don't figure things out in life until we see the replay or get the do-over—not that every opportunity comes with a do-over. Sometimes things don't make sense immediately, but eventually they do. Back when I was in high school, I had a decision to make: go to a smaller college and continue to play soccer or go to Boston College and get a business degree. I was destroyed by indecision—play sports or attend one of the top business schools in the country? There was not an option that allowed me to do both. I had no idea what to do. I was so conflicted it tore me up; I decided to go to Boston College, but it felt like I was giving up on my dreams in sports.

My mom saw me struggling with the decision I had even as I was packing to leave for college, so she decided to take me to a local religious woman who was rumored to be a prophet. I think my mother thought the prophet would make me feel more comfortable, more at ease with my choice to go to Boston College.

My mom and I entered this room, and sat down, and the prophet pulled out a deck of angel cards and told me to shuffle them while keeping my questions in mind. As I shuffled, I could feel her watching me, and I thought, *How could this possibly answer my questions? She doesn't know me.*

As soon as the thought entered my mind, she put her hand on mine and said, "You have quite a few guardian angels watching you, you have a very special path." I was suddenly at peace. It was as if, just in her touch, she had relieved me of the stress and tension I had carried into her space.

Without reorganizing the cards, she turned two over, then asked, "Why did you leave your path in sports?"

"I chose to go to business school instead."

She closed her eyes and said, "That is a detour from your destined path."

My mom's eyes widened in shock. It wasn't exactly the answer she'd been hoping we'd hear.

"You are fighting for what you think is the smart decision," the prophet said, "but it's not your path, that's why you are so uncertain."

As if she felt the gravity of her words hit my spirit, she reached for my hand again. Again, I felt almost high with the peace that washed over me. "This is a detour," she said, "but not an end. To follow your path, you will have to leave the money."

The words echoed in my mind. I had convinced myself that perfect pumps and a penthouse were worth trading in my cleats. I felt like I was selling out, but in a way that was part of growing up. Then, I was being told that my angels were not happy because I was detouring from my path and that I could get back onto my path only by leaving the money? This lady had to be crazy. She had to be wrong. I wanted her to be wrong, even though I felt the truth in her touch and in her words.

She answered my doubts when she said, "I know I will not change your mind now, but when you feel stuck in your life, I want you to remember that to find your way back to your path in sports, to live your destiny, you will have to leave the money."

The idea of leaving money terrified me. I wanted money. I wanted the security associated with it.

She smiled. "You have the chance to do something no one else can, but you have to be willing to sacrifice to do it. Follow that path through with faith, and you will be rewarded at the end of your journey."

I ignored her initially, and attended business school. But her words never left me. Years later, I was able to understand that the experience taught me to always be open to learning a lesson, even if it feels too late.

A Second (and Third) Chance at Playing Big

At Boston College I found rugby. It was the closest thing I had ever seen to football that women were playing. Maybe I could stay on my path after all? So, I jumped in, and I was really good. I even got a chance to try out for the national team, but I was promptly and painfully told, once again, that I was too small to play. It stirred up all of those tennis feelings; it cut me to the core. After I graduated, like tennis, I put rugby behind me.

I got an adult job, with an adult paycheck, but my love for sports was still strong. I taught aerobics before and after work, and I played flag football on weekends. When I got a call to try out for the Massachusetts Mutiny, a women's professional football team, for one slim second, I had a tennis flashback—I almost let that fear of being too small stop me. But, pretty quickly, my confidence surged and I agreed to give it a shot. Yet, as the date of the tryout approached, doubt inched back in. The night before, my size hurdle dominated my mind, and my old rejections played out. *What if they tell me I'm too small?* That would sure fit the pattern.

I'd loved football my entire life. Now I was so close to being able to play it myself, and yet that proximity scared me. What if the love of my life ended in rejection? Could I handle that?

Consider the fork in the road I was facing: I could continue to earn a tidy living working in my corporate job, or I could step into my destiny. I had that big job with that big paycheck and that fancy apartment one block from Fenway, but should I leave it all for sports, even if I might not make the team? As I fretted over that decision, the words of the prophet from years earlier echoed in my mind. Deep down, I had always known that to follow my path I would have to leave the money. As a teen, I thought that woman was crazy. But suddenly, with football in my future, her prophecy was clear, though my path was anything but.

Finally, I came to a pivotal decision. I could live with being too small; after all, I had lived with it my whole life. What I could not live with was missing my chance and always wondering what would have happened if I had just tried out for that football team. I had to do it.

And, with no road map to follow, I quit my job, took the risk of a lifetime, and stepped into my destiny.

But what would have happened had I never tried out for that football team? Fear of rejection could have kept me from my destiny of becoming one of the best woman players in the game, one who played for fifteen years and won four World Championships, one who won two gold medals and who then made history in men's professional football. Look what happened because I *did* go to that tryout. I hold this lesson close to my heart always. I urge you to remember it any time you need a little courage to try when you fear failure.

I gave up my cushy job and moved back home to Florida with my parents so I could prepare full time for my football tryout.

COACH JEN: THE ROAD TO SUCCESS IS PAVED WITH SACRIFICE

To be able to take this shot, I slashed my bills and let go of my fancy apartment. I had some savings, and I was willing to use that money to go for it. This was the chance of a lifetime. I'm not telling you to quit your job tomorrow if you have bills and a mortgage and kids. That's not responsible. I had more flexibility than most people in that respect. But you can take steps so your dream eventually materializes:

- First, make sure you are financially prepared to make a transition or plan to save for when your opportunity arises. Assess the financial risks of chasing a dream—will it cost you money? What does that do to your long- and short-term finances? Can you afford it? You need backing, savings, a budget, and a financial forecast. Seek help if you can't provide them yourself. →

- Assess your current situation and figure out when you can carve out time in your week to chase your dream. Do it. Make the time. Even an hour a week is a huge step.

- Consider the nonfinancial implications: Does it affect your current job or your family? Identify the weak points in your plan and figure out how you have to navigate them.

- Remember: You might not need to commit full time to your pursuit. If you want to sing or write or paint or run a marathon, you can do all of these things on the side; you just have to schedule and time it right.

- Don't be in a rush to commit for the sake of committing. I heard the prophet but didn't act on her advice until a full decade after she uttered the words.

The Moment the Tables Turned

My sister came with me to the Mass Mutiny tryout. We walked into the gym for the indoor portion and looked around at the other women there vying for a spot. One of the first players we ran into was Sue Burtoft. She was built, solid, and standing at about five-eleven or so. She looked like a tight end. My sister grabbed my arm and said, "Jenny, are you sure you want to do this?"

I looked at her and said, "Oh, yeah, absolutely."

My fear wasn't about Sue Burtoft or my ability. It was about their telling me I was too little. I had felt defeat before thanks to my size. Defying that insecurity hadn't been an easy task. Even though there was an enormous risk to my ego and my self-confidence in taking the field that day to try out, I had made a decision. I'd never stopped thinking about what would have happened if I'd ignored that tennis coach and pursued tennis. The regret had stuck with me for half a lifetime, and I wasn't about to let the same thing happen with my football dream.

I pushed that insecurity way down deep so when I got my shot at open tryout . . . I nailed it. I was immediately in love with the feeling of being on that field; I had found my home. Size, this time, was not going to get in my way. I was playing big, shutting out all that doubt, all those naysayers in my life—for good. It struck me: "This is it. This is where I'm meant to be." I had no doubt. I had no idea about how or why or any of the details, but I just knew I was meant to be in football. I could feel it with every fiber of my being. There I was. That day at tryouts I had not even a flicker of uncertainty that I had edged my way in despite the odds.

At five-foot-two, 130 pounds, I made the Mass Mutiny women's football team. All those misgivings about being too small washed away. All the nerves settled. I was beside myself with joy—my lifetime love of football was no longer just a distant dream.

COACH JEN:
WHAT DOES PLAYING BIG MEAN FOR YOU?

- It's your vibe that you bring to every situation—your chemistry.

- It's the message that you send by the character you demonstrate.

- It's not how big you are, it's how big you play.

- You can have a big impact on a team, not by being the biggest player but by being a force with your presence. Ultimately, the impact that you can have on a team is bigger than your own physical limitations.

To Find Your Way,
You Will Have to Leave the Money

I had definitely given up the money. There was nothing glamorous about being a pro football player in the women's league. We played real eleven-on-eleven, smashmouth, NFL-rules football. Most of us had several day jobs. It was work by day and play football by night. We were all passion, no paycheck. Many days, I felt like I was being held together by duct tape, but you would never catch me coming out of a game because I chipped my toenail polish. That was the life of women in football. It's also the life of anyone who is living that full-time hustle, fully committed to chasing a dream.

Only as a luxury did we ride in beat-up yellow school buses to our games. Most times, we piled into cars and drove ourselves there. We were trying to learn and practice and often had to do so indoors in gyms, and if we did get outside, we faced some truly terrible field conditions. We would shovel snow off our own practice fields or clear the rocks, garbage, and used syringes from the park areas we practiced in. That image of everybody's pulling their cars up close and shining their headlights on the field— that wasn't just something from the movies. That was how we squeezed in extra practices at night.

In my second year with the Mass Mutiny, the lack of financial backing and back-office support became even more painful. I was not only a player but also the marketing department. All of us had off-the-field jobs supporting the team. It's just how it was. We had to market ourselves by putting up flyers and posters all over the place, and we had to sell tickets to our own games— whatever it took to fill the stands. There was no other option. We were fighting to stay on the field, and although it was frustrating, it was what it was. There was no magic money (even though we were pro!) that allowed us to simply focus on football. We had real jobs by day and football dreams by night.

None of this stopped us, though. We were living our dream. Year after year, the struggle deepened on every single level. Still, we played big. Bigger together and as big as humanly possible.

Play Your Own Game, but Play It Big

When I first became a football player, I had this idea of what that had to look like: I wore all black; I didn't smile because I was supposed to be tough; I thought I should lift really heavy weights so I could get bigger. But as I got bigger, I lost some of my speed and agility. I finally realized that I wasn't going to be able to out-big anybody on the field size-wise, but I didn't need to play their game. I needed to own my game and embrace my skills, style, and attitude: I could out-little and out-crazy them. Once I owned my unique style and embraced my size, I took my game to a much higher level.

Early in my career (and many times later) I heard, "Look at this cute little linebacker." At first, it pissed me off. I thought *cute* and *little* were insults, and in the context of football, they pretty much were. But one day I realized those insults could actually be the secrets to my success. I played up those stereotypes, and played with my opponents' minds in the process. That was one way I played big.

I intimidated people in my own way, despite my size. I figured out how to play up my strengths in a way that had the biggest impact. I wore makeup when I played. I always put my hair in pigtail braids. I wore pink shoelaces in my shoes and a pink undershirt. Cute, yup. And then I would tackle the largest girl on the field, offer her help up, and say with a smile, "Baby, do you need a hand? 'Cause I'm going to be here all day." That was my bigness.

In my office—that football field—I found the strength to defy the preconceived notions. I played and looked and acted my own way, and that was a good thing. I owned what I had to offer. I crafted my own special sauce of bigness.

Through that, I learned about my impact on the game over-all. It wasn't just about the play I made, it was about everything I did between plays. I had the ability to change people's view of me; they were watching not just the play but also what happened afterward: Did I walk off the field head up and shoulders back or head down? Did I make eye contact? Did I have swag? Did I have attitude?

This transcends sports: your mind and body are connected in everything you do. That's the way somebody judges you and the way you judge others. Eye contact suggests confidence, which suggests bigness. Shoulders back and head up suggest that, too. Your brain interprets your physical behavior and decides for you that you're confident. And other people's brains pick up on that, too, and they think, *She's confident and she has a big presence.*

You can change how people see you by adjusting the way you interact, react, and carry yourself. Once you make small changes in one area of your life, those behaviors carry over into others un-til your winning attitude becomes consistent in all areas of your life. In essence, you're creating a character and nailing it at all points of intersection in your world. And if you do that, you're playing big.

When a guy is good at many things, we think of him as being a Renaissance man—the guy who is good at everything. It's an endearing term. There's no equivalent term or accounting for a woman who is good at everything. Probably because the women back in the Renaissance were wearing corsets and they therefore weren't able to do anything because they weren't able to breathe. Today, there is that same restrictive thinking—we have to basically free ourselves from our corsets and step into our own greatness, which, for most of us, has many dimensions. As we free ourselves from restrictions, we change not only how men view women but how women view themselves.

2

Be an *And,* Not an *Or*

So often in life women are taught to be just one thing. You learn that lesson early on and carry it through to adulthood. You don't realize that what makes you different makes you special. You don't have to categorize yourself—you can do and be many things. Whether at work or at home, it's too easy to get caught in a singular effort, under pressure to conform to one label. I am here to tell you that's not the case. Be an and, not an or.

AS IMPORTANT AS it is to find your game, that thing that lights you up like football does for me, and to play it big, you should never forget that being multifaceted is a good thing.

Who you are is not solely defined by what you do. This is the balancing act of life. Obviously, excellence requires hard work and laser focus; however, even the most dedicated of performers have facets of their life outside of their chosen field. After all, the day has twenty-four hours, and no one can practice twenty-four hours a day. For me, playing football is a component of who I am, so I don't simply say, "I play football." I say, "I am a football player." However, who I am, my sense of self, includes many other "I am's." I am a PhD. I am a sister, a daughter, a writer, an artist, a runner, a terrible cook, a great friend, an animal lover, and more.

You get my point. I am not entirely defined by one aspect of myself. Yes, you may dedicate a great deal of your time to the pursuit of excellence in your particular game, but it is important to realize that you are more than that pursuit. Think of a diamond. The true brilliance is revealed as the stone is cut to capture the light with multiple facets, freeing that inner fire and sparkle. You have the same brilliant, beautiful dimensions, so own your facets and shine. If you're an ass-kicking lawyer *and* a poet in your spare time, channel that energy you use to power through at work and schedule time to write your poems with that same force and focus. Then share your work—with family, friends, or strangers on social media. Start a poetry blog or join a group. But don't hide that secret passion or skill.

I didn't know when I was young that it was okay to stand out. It took becoming an adult and living through more tests of my individuality to have that realization. As a kid, I didn't know that being an *and* was better than being an *or*. In fact, my epiphany about being multifaceted and possessing multiple skills was fifteen years in the making. It was a very long time before I realized it's good to be different. Not just good—amazing.

I'm glad I figured it out. Being an *and* is the precise reason I was hired to be a coach in the NFL.

WHEN I THINK back, the pressure to commit to just one element of myself didn't start at birth—it was taught. In sixth grade, with my competitive nature I was fearless in my quest for greatness. I saw no conflict in being multidimensional. I starred in the school play, competed in academic games, and was a talented athlete. I believed I could be good at everything, and I worked hard at all of it. But, as it does for many girls, somehow that belief faded. Middle school's about the age when confidence and pride at standing out start to dwindle and desire to squeeze into society's preconceived notions of what we should be like or look like and how we should act starts to invade. Consciousness of judgment sneaks in there in the early teen years. It develops. It's not inherent.

Like most kids, I went from taking pride in standing out to desperately wanting to fit in. I started to see boxes and definitions of who I was supposed to be. That's what happens: we start labeling kids and kids then learn to label each other and themselves. And by doing that, by boxing people into one category, labeling becomes limiting.

I didn't understand at the time, but at some point being cool became more important than being the best at everything I could. Suddenly, being the best wasn't cool.

In sixth grade, I was number two in the county in math. And I was mad that I wasn't number one. Over time, though, maybe because it was no longer cool to win, or maybe because I was protecting myself out of fear that I couldn't win, I started to resent and push back against the good-at-math label. By ninth grade, instead of focusing on being the best at math, I was intent on providing comic relief. When I had to buckle down and work hard, I did, but I didn't come off as a serious person all the time. I was trying to find my place, like everybody else. When we'd travel to a math competition, instead of being proud of what I was doing, I started sitting toward the back of the bus, saying things like, "Are we really doing this?"

In tenth grade I was placed in a math class for top students—the ones who, like me, had been competing in academic competitions. Though I used to thrive in math, suddenly the special class and associated competitions felt like obligations. An uninspired participant, I did not take it seriously. You could say I created a self-fulfilling prophecy because teachers no longer considered me among their top prospects, either.

On the first day of that advanced class, the teacher gave us a six-question test, all extremely difficult questions. Getting a six would be an accomplishment. We handed in our tests and the teacher graded them on the spot without looking at the names as she marked them up. Once she was finished, she handed them out by announcing each person's name and score.

"Carrie, you got six, congratulations. Chandra, you got a five, amazing."

It went on like that, and for anybody who scored above four, the teacher piled on sincere accolades.

Then she pulled out my test. "Jen." She looked a bit confused. "Jen, you got a six," she said with her Southern accent. Then she looked at me. "How'd you do that?" She was shocked that I did well, and she made that clear to everyone. She said it out loud in front of the entire class.

I thought, *So, it's like that? That's how it's going to be?* At that moment, I decided I no longer wanted to do the work. I didn't want to be called out for having a top score. I didn't want my academic strengths not to make sense to people, thanks to how they had labeled me in their head. That teacher had assumed I was this or that, a jokester maybe, or an athlete, but clearly not a math whiz. She had labeled me and limited me at the same time.

She went on to tell us that we could miss or fail any test throughout the semester, but if we got an A on the final, which was guaranteed to be excruciatingly hard, she would give us an A for the class.

Her initial underestimation of me produced a negative reaction: it generated attitude within me. I simply stopped trying. I tuned out. I lashed back. In my mind, I thought it would hurt her if I hurt myself. She'd made her opinion of me public, and, somehow, I would force her to experience the side of me she had expected. It wasn't a savvy plan. If you had asked me then whether I was insecure, I would have said no. But her words cut into something that compelled me to make that shift.

Fortunately, even though I blew off most of the year, by the time that final exam came around, I had summoned back my fire and competitive spirit. That little girl who was number two in the county in academic games, the pride of the math competition circuit, decided to show up and show that teacher what I was capable of. For that, I'm grateful: I was able to save myself. I decided that I'd made my point all semester long, but on that final I was getting my A back.

I took that final. And I got my A. She handed the test back to me on the last day of class. A giant A was scrawled at the top, which meant I got an A in the class, too. I looked at it, looked at her, nodded, and walked out. *I got you*. I proved her wrong—her label was inaccurate. I was an *and*.

When I transferred schools the following year, yet again my reputation preceded me. The first day of math class, the teacher addressed the class. "You better be the smartest kids in the school, because this is the hardest class."

I started to get up, saying, "I must be in the wrong room."

"Sit down," he said. "Ms. Welter, I was warned about you."

COACH JEN: ON STEM

To be sure, my math experience was also a sign of the times. Today, there's at least a push to get girls studying science and math, but back then, these were traditionally masculine subjects that girls weren't encouraged to join. The push for girls in Science, Technology, Engineering, and Mathematics (STEM) now is significant; even so, we haven't moved the needle enough.

According to Change the Equation, an organization helping to increase students' STEM literacy, a surge in the number of STEM jobs is expected. And yet, according to Girls Who Code, a national nonprofit dedicated to closing the gender gap in technology, although girls in middle school express interest in STEM studies in vast numbers, by high school, only 0.4 percent choose computer science as a college major. Somewhere along the way, girls are losing interest, or losing steam. A girl who excels in math or who makes it in Silicon Valley these days is still the exception, not the rule. In 2015, women made up nearly half the workforce but held less than 10 percent of tech jobs.

Interestingly, though not the norm for that era, my math team was mostly girls. We were stacked with smart girls—ahead of our time, for certain. In fact, a girl named Leah, who was always getting sixes on those tests, is now a math professor. She's a brilliant woman, and she rocked the math team, but traditionally, she was an exception. Then again, I was a statistic—one of those girls who lost interest. It was hard for us to be rocking math and be girls. And that's a problem we've still got to fight today.

Stop Putting People in Boxes

We do it far too often: categorize people. We put them in boxes in terms of how we see them or how we define them. To fix that thinking, we first need to differentiate areas where it's appropriate to compete from those where it's not. For example, beauty is not a competition. There are many ways to be beautiful. Just because someone else is beautiful doesn't make you less beautiful. The label of *beautiful* isn't assigned to only one of us.

On my eighteenth birthday, which was a very cool day, I was named to the homecoming court at my high school. As a girl who never wore makeup and instead wore athletic shorts and a ponytail every single day, this nomination came as a complete shock. I didn't consider myself traditionally pretty; clearly, my classmates saw me differently.

Still, I stepped out of my comfort zone and enlisted the help of a neighbor before the homecoming parade. She fixed my hair and did a glamorous job of my makeup. When I showed up in a floor-length black gown, everyone was astounded. Apparently, there had been a running bet that I'd arrive in a ponytail, soccer shorts, and T-shirt. Once again, I had been put in a box. In high school, I kept all of the components of myself separate, but we must encourage girls—and our fellow women—not to.

COACH JEN:
FIVE WAYS TO BE FREE TO BE AN *AND*

How do we avoid boxing ourselves and our kids in?

1. *Champion being multidimensional:* Celebrate greatness in various dimensions as well as the process of becoming great. Don't let one skill define you; one aspect of your life shouldn't be your entire identity. Be great at as many things as possible and share and show people all of your wonderful facets.

2. *Highlight the achievements of others:* Realize that some- one else's greatness does not diminish yours. Are diamonds diminished by the beauty of rubies? Of course not, so don't be afraid to show that you are beautiful and intelligent and smart and an athlete and an artist and everything you can be, and don't be shy about telling the world. If you accom- plish something, share your triumphs, own your brilliance, step past the line of normalcy, of expectations, and of ceil- ings that try to define and at times diminish you. As you push past perceived limitations, you inspire others to push past theirs.

3. *Laugh at yourself:* Own the awkward. It often takes feeling awkward and uncomfortable to develop talent. When was the last time you let yourself be really bad at something? There is freedom in being bad at something, so challenge yourself to embrace failure. Most of us have trained our- selves to stay in a safe, relatively judgment-free bubble where we spend our time focused on things we're good or even great at. In the process, our ego gets so protec- tive that we shy away from trying things we fear we might

fail at. Time to own failure, put your ego on a timeout, throw perfection out the window, challenge your comfort zone, and do something you think you will be terrible at. Fear of judgment from others and from ourselves keeps us trapped. When you find fun and humor in learning, it helps reinvigorate your adventurous spirit. Sometimes failures bring freedom.

4. *Embrace your inner child:* Remember being a kid, looking up at the clouds, and watching a story emerge in the shapes—one with no limits and no judgment? As you grew up, the opportunities to look up at the sky and dream likely were replaced with obligations. Tap into your pure curiosity and joy, free from the pressure of an end goal. Have you always wanted to take an improv class or learn to play the trumpet? Have you always been curious about a subject but believed it didn't fit with who you were? Do something whimsical. Sign up for that crazy class. Set aside one hour a week to shoot hoops in the park or play hopscotch or do something that gave you joy when you were young. We spend so much time focused on getting to that one goal—the degree, the job, the house, the husband—that we forget our inner child wants to have fun. Fun opens our minds and breaks down the boxes and labels.

Identity Foreclosure

The flip side of embracing multiple talents and dimensions of yourself is something we often discuss in sport psychology known as identity foreclosure. When an athlete experiences identity foreclosure, he or she has locked into being *only* that athlete. The danger of locking our identity into only one aspect of ourselves leads to burnout, injury, or an end to that sense of self. If the key to your identity, and in turn your confidence, resides entirely in one "I am," when that aspect of your identity is jeopardized or evolves, often a loss of self or an identity crisis occurs.

For example, it's much easier to transition out of one job or career path when we embrace multiple dimensions of ourselves. We can be a mom, a daughter, an athlete, a corporate executive, and an artist. People who identify with being all sorts of things are less likely to lose themselves if one element disappears from their makeup.

If you can consider all the various pieces of you, not just the one that consumes most of your time, you'll find it easier to avoid identity foreclosure. You can reinvent your time and your timing. You can find many new places in the world where you'll excel. Whether in your organization, in your personal development, or at the intersection of these, feeding passions amplifies life satisfaction. That's a key to happiness: accept and own that you were blessed with multiple gifts for a reason.

IF YOU'RE STRUGGLING with how to see this, imagine you're talking to your daughter: What would you say to encourage her to be all she can be? Would you ever say, "Only be smart. Don't also be pretty. Don't also be a dancer. Don't also learn to play guitar"? No. You'd embrace every unique and special thing about her and applaud all her pieces.

Remember that labels stick. With labels that categorize people, that emphasize being an *or,* we take away their fairy tales and shift them toward real lives with real (perceived or otherwise) limits. We teach them that boxes do exist. And that they need to fit in them.

Instead, if she wants to wear two different colored socks, let her. If she wants to take dance class even though she has no moves, let her. If she wants to learn something new even though it's not her strongest subject, encourage it all. Don't tell her what she is. Let her be everything.

Then go ahead and love yourself as much as you love your daughter.

COACH JEN:
FREE YOURSELF TO FIND YOURSELF

- *Channel fearlessness:* Be inquisitive and brave in everything you do. Be that wonderfully fearless, curious child you once were by freeing yourself of all of those limiting adult lessons.

- *Free yourself from restrictive thinking:* Don't strive for the top job or the cutting-edge accomplishment in your field—think beyond that. What if you could go further? What would that look like? Can you see it? There's no path to where you want to go—can you envision the new one?

- *Free yourself from fear:* We have all let fear stop us in our tracks. I know I have. But whenever I did, I at least tried to unmask it. Ask yourself, what am I really afraid of? Think of the fear like a monster under your bed: If you have never seen it, how do you know what's really there? The hardest part is being willing to actually look at your fear. Too

→

many times, fear can keep you paralyzed. If you've pulled the sheets over your head, it's impossible to see what you need to do. Sometimes it's the execution, not the result, that scares us. For example, you don't want to be in your current relationship, but you're terrified to end it. Think of the other side—maybe it's not being alone that scares you but rather the act of ending the relationship. In any situation try to break down what exactly you fear. But don't let that fear cause you to do nothing at all; take on the hardest part first. Remember, you are never alone, so ask for help facing the monster. Find someone with a flashlight who will hold your hand and help you look at the problem.

- *Free yourself from feeling like you're going to be judged:* Dismiss all those adages you were told growing up about speaking only when spoken to and waiting your turn. Speak up. Interject. Your point might not be 100 percent on the mark, but it might spark an idea in your group or show that you are more than, say, an accountant or bookkeeper or office manager.

- *Free yourself from focusing on what other people are doing—especially when it invalidates what you're doing:* There's a famous saying: "Comparison is the thief of joy." You can't measure your success by comparing your path or results to those of others. Keep your eyes on your own progress and measure it by your standards.

Once you're free, you'll find yourself and you'll find the people who will truly have your back in all of your many endeavors.

Painting is another good example. I ignored my love for art for a long time, in part because my mom was an art teacher and my sister is an exceptional artist—she went to the Rhode Island School of Design. The funny part is that Rachel was also a gifted athlete and model. Like with tennis, I was always thinking that I couldn't be good at the same things as her—not true.

Later in my life, Randy Jacobs, a talented artist and a good friend, taught me about his style of painting. I was so inspired by his teaching. After many years of leaving that skill to my mom and sister, I found an escape in painting. I'm not competitive as an artist. I just do it for joy. And that's my point: one of my epiphanies was to realize that I didn't have to be a world-renowned artist to make art one of my things. I could be at the top of my game in one aspect of my life, but that didn't mean my painting, for example, had to be as good as my football. I used to think it did.

This faulty thinking was evident back in math class in high school. Then, worry and self-doubt translated into an attitude toward the teacher, but maybe I was worried my math skills wouldn't be as good as my soccer skills. If you aren't the prettiest girl in the room, are you still pretty? Yeah, of course you are. You are pretty in your own unique way, and somebody else's shine does not diminish yours. Maybe thinking it's a zero-sum game is the fear that stops us, though.

Being an *and* was actually the number one reason that I made it to the NFL. Early in my professional football career, I had pursued my master's degree because I wanted to be able to learn more about sports and psychology. Later, because women in football weren't getting paid, I thought that if I earned my doctorate, I would be able to merge my practical experience with theoretical knowledge and create a unique way to contribute. Ultimately, I obtained a master's degree in sport psychology and a

PhD in psychology by balancing my laptop on my knees on the long bus trips to away games. While other people were having fun or reviewing the playbook, I was studying. It was not the popular choice, but it was my choice. I knew I was a great football player, and I wanted to achieve greatness in academics as well.

People called me crazy, but in 2013 when my dissertation was published, I became the insanely unique combination of a football-playing doctor. I was the ultimate *and*; no longer living in fear of not fitting in, I wanted to stand out.

That mentality and the need for varying skills relate to today's workforce: technology is forcing our world to move so quickly now. Faster than ever before. We all have to keep up and learn to shift into different roles as the work world grows and changes. In corporate America, we're working harder with fewer resources. If you are an *and,* you might get a chance at something unexpected because you know more and have a long list of *and*s. This makes you a supervaluable employee—one who can fit into different and new departments and roles—and create your own.

In forward-thinking places like Silicon Valley, the boxes and the lines between job roles? Well, they're going away. Companies aren't defining positions as much as they are letting employees self-manage and pursue avenues according to ability. The world is changing and therefore the traditional way of working is no longer the only way. Being an *and* is currency in the changing marketplace and global economy.

I didn't fully realize exactly how well the *and* notion would pay off for me until Arizona Cardinals head coach Bruce Arians entered my life. I was a coach and a player, and I had earned a PhD in psychology. When Bruce did his research on me, and when he spoke to me or about me, the conversation wasn't only about football. It was about the integration of theory and practice—my on-the-field skill coupled with my education. He asked me about my doctorate and the ways that he thought it would enhance my ability to relate to the guys in the locker room. His philosophy surrounding my hire had to do with his opinion that great coaches start by being great teachers. He has been quoted as saying, "Coaching is nothing more than teaching. One thing I have learned from players is 'How are you going to make me better? If you can make me better, I don't care if you're the Green Hornet, I'll listen.'" In other words, if you can reach them, you can teach them. That's where my psychology background came into play. It was the differentiating factor for me, the thing that opened the door.

I'm asking you to practice something that I didn't practice until later in my life, long after I'd made the mistake of hiding my other talents, so I understand how difficult this can be. But being an *and* can pay off big time.

Professionalism is not defined by the dollars you make. It is the attitude you take.

||||||||||||||||||||||||||||||||||||||||||||||||||||||||||||||||||||||||||||||||||||

3

Play Priceless

> Remember that winning and success are not absolute terms. They are relative and very personal. Winning can be the outcome of a competition, but it can also be the opportunity to compete despite the odds. Success is a personal philosophy based on your metrics of victory. It is not what someone else defines for you, but what you define for yourself. To be a professional in your game is about your attitude toward a situation and the value you assign to yourself, not the salary someone assigns to you. When you define your systems of measurement, values, and worth, then you truly define your power and how you are going to live your life.

A SINGLE DOLLAR never meant so much as it did when I played pro women's football.

After two years with the Mutiny, I played one season with the Dallas Dragons before joining the Dallas Diamonds. In 2004, my Diamonds team went undefeated in the regular season, and we won our first Women's Professional Football League (WPFL) Super Bowl. That win marked the beginning of a dynasty: the

Diamonds would go on to three more championships over the next four years. But it marked something else as well: the first time I was paid to play football, the sport I had loved since I was a kid. I was officially a professional football player.

At the end-of-year ceremony that season, we were each awarded our women's league version of a Super Bowl ring and given a profit-sharing check for $12, which amounted to exactly $1 per game. So meaningful and significant was that check that I never cashed it. That was back in the days before you could make a deposit using your iPhone and then keep the paper check. Back then, once the paper check went in the machine or to the teller, it was gone forever. That check meant more to me than $12 so I kept it. It was an important reminder of what we were all playing for.

The profit sharing never exceeded $1 per game, despite the Diamonds' dominance in the sport. At our peak, that Diamonds dynasty, well, it was the best women's football ever was. Several thousand fans filled the stands at our games, and on occasion that number surged closer to seven thousand. Still, those fans were paying only $10 a ticket, and no major endorsers invested in us.

Our profit sharing was symbolic at best. Each player actually had to pay to play, from our own wallets or from some other source. We had to generate some kind of sponsorship to the tune of $1,000 each. Even though we were referred to as professional football players, I chose to say "pro" because we couldn't afford all those extra letters. We certainly didn't have the financial backing of the NFL. We were like high school sports teams that raised money to play in all sorts of ways, including through local sponsors—we're not talking Gatorade or anything here. In fact, many high school teams were dramatically better funded than we were. The WNBA, which had taken off by this time, was substantially better funded; it couldn't even be compared to our league because it had NBA backing. Being treated like the WNBA would have been a serious upgrade. We all dreamed of a nod from the NFL.

COACH JEN:
WHAT DOES SUCCESS LOOK LIKE?

- Make sure you never confuse money with security, and comfort with progress. Success doesn't always come with a big paycheck. Your worth is not defined by what someone pays you. My team's budget was $12, but my worth was priceless.

- You are the author of your life. What really matters is that you feel successful and fulfilled.

- Focus on what you can control, which is *you*. You cannot control the approval of others. You cannot measure your success by gauging the feelings of others. You cannot live your life for other people's approval or to fulfill their dreams.

- Success is not an objective standard, nor is it a static target.

- Constantly evaluate where you are relative to what you are capable of. Use that as your true metric of success.

- Find small successes in moments, within relationships, with progress, and along the journey. The grand finale and its reward aren't the only measures of success. A small win in a day, such as someone's answering your call, is a success. Landing the job you're calling about is a larger success, but not the only one.

And yet, left to our own devices and through sheer hustle, we did what we had to do, fund-raising in any way possible. We held car washes and sought out personal player sponsorships. There was a prevailing mentality that we were all in it together. If one person quickly raised her $1,000, she would jump in to help another player raise hers. We worked together to make sure that everyone could play and that nobody had to step down because she couldn't raise the funds. Sometimes players got lucky if an individual would back them and pay their sponsorship, but that was rare.

Eventually, a businesswoman named Susan Mead covered me and did so for years. She was like a guardian angel who helped me stay in the game.

Even a Winning Team Was a Broke Team

The brokeness of our Diamonds team made the circumstances tough; scrambling and shoddy conditions were the norm, not the exception. Remember that movie *Major League*? It was a lot like that—even as champions it was about as rough as you could imagine, almost like we were being tested to see how much we could endure and if we would crack.

Long Beach, California, turned out to be a potential breaking point. Rather than enduring an endless bus ride, we flew in from Dallas, but the joy of that splurge was damned when we arrived at the skankiest, dumpiest, oldest, most rundown motel any of us had ever seen. Trust me, we didn't expect much, but this was a new low, even for women's football. The place was falling apart, paint-chipped doors, the whole thing. It was a nightmare from the outside, but we briefly held out hope that inside the rooms would somehow redeem themselves.

We were mistaken. We typically slept four to a room. My foursome got our key, unlocked the door, and entered. The room was dark and dirty and it smelled like old feet. Looking back, I can see that keeping the room dark would have been the best strategy so that we didn't see just how totally disgusting it was. Even in the dark, it was clear the room hadn't been cleaned, and none of us was eager to have a blue light shone in there to see what lurked. Within seconds of walking in, we did a U-turn right back out to regroup.

In contrast to the dingy room, it was a beautiful day outside. Still in our travel gear (having made a conscious choice not to change, unpack, or leave our bags in the room), a few of us gathered around the pool. Eventually, the majority of the team did the same, and within a short time, dozens of us were poolside trying to make the best of a bad situation, enjoy the California weather, and decompress ahead of our game. No such luck.

We immediately had what one might call an "Oh, damn" moment. The front desk guy stormed out and started yelling at us, telling us we had to leave the pool area. We were bewildered. Did he expect us to sit in our rooms, as dreadful as they were? Amid the chaos, we learned that we were, in fact, occupying the territory where the prostitutes sat to pick up their johns. Because we were football players, apparently we were intimidating the girls, who didn't feel comfortable asking us to move or share space. We were bad for business. We joked about making that our new fund-raising opportunity, but that obviously wasn't happening. He chased us out.

This was the one and only time our owner pulled us from a hotel because it was simply too bad, even for our budget. The next hotel was average, but when you're upgrading from abysmal—so abysmal you can't even sit on the bed—anything was a welcomed improvement. We certainly weren't complaining.

Sometimes, we weren't even given rooms at all. The trip to New Orleans was one experience like no other. We were excited to go to the Big Easy. To save money, the owner thought it would be a great idea if we took the bus down, played our game, showered at the field, and then hit Bourbon Street. Because it was a place that stayed open all night long for partying, our owner decided once we'd had our fun, we could just head back to the bus and sleep on the way home. No hotel was factored into the equation. This wasn't something we voted on or collectively decided. It was a directive handed down by the owner.

COACH JEN: THE TEAM MENTALITY

How to handle being poorly managed: If you're not loving the way you or your team is being managed, I suggest you step up and manage yourself. Look at a given situation, evaluate how you can contribute, and work toward providing those contributions. If you have leadership talents that are not being utilized (and I bet you do), then you need to make those talents known to others any way you can.

How to manage a group: Know the group from the bottom up and know the vision of that group from the top down. Any good team should have an overall goal or vision, shared by everyone. As a leader, it's your job to create group buy-in and individual buy-in. To create buy-in, you should put each individual in the position where that person can provide the maximum impact. As a leader, you should connect with each individual and understand him or her as a person and as a contributor, then tap into his or her personal talents and personality attributes. That will maximize your team's contribution and create synergy for the overall vision.

The New Orleans plan turned out to be incredibly flawed, and our trip to the Big Easy was anything but. To start with, it was the worst bus ride we'd ever experienced. In the dead heat of summer, with sixty-some people (coaches and players) on board, Dallas to New Orleans, passing through every gross hot zone possible—sticky, humid, and hot—the air conditioning broke. And this wasn't one of those luxury charters where we could have spread out a bit. No, this was a basic bus, and our seating was two-by-two. We were packed right up against our neighbors, sticky, sweaty skin and all.

By the time we got to New Orleans, every last one of us was smelly, disgusting, and cranky. We felt like we had actually melted, but we still had to go out and play a football game.

Now, back in Texas, most of the high school football fields we played on were nice. In Allen, Texas, for example, we played on a $60 million field. Even our home field was well kept, with seating for ten thousand people. It was gorgeous. Other than a college or pro field, there was no nicer field we could have asked to play on. So we were a little spoiled by our home field.

In Texas, high school football is big business and big money. In New Orleans, not so much. We got to the field, and it was, essentially, a community park. There were bleachers, not stadium seats. Run-of-the-mill regular aluminum bleachers, and not even a lot of them. Add to that a chain-link fence around the perimeter and, though we were used to playing on turf, the field was grass, and not great grass but lumpy clods with dirt patches in between.

We shouldn't have been surprised, therefore, that the locker room closely resembled the set of a prison movie. The shower room was an open-air cinderblock enclosure with a few rusty spigots. And I say *room*, but I mean *wall*, because the shower area was simply set behind the chain-link fence whose gate was held shut with a rusty old lock. There was one drain in the middle of the space, and off to the side, a tiny changing area that barely more than two or three of us could fit into at once.

In a traditional season, we started out with fifty-five or so players, like the men's teams did, but after injuries or people quitting, the team would often be whittled down to about forty people. When our team was at the top of the league—when we were really, really good—we had about sixty players. So, there we were: sixty cranky, sweaty, tired players and a cell block shower and skimpy changing space. This was a low point for sure. Not one person dared to shower. Aside from how exposed it was, we felt certain we would catch something. Because we traveled in such close quarters, we had a must-shower rule. On this day, we flipped the rule: Nobody was to enter that shower.

Despite the conditions, we played that game and we kicked their asses. The owner had booked two motel rooms for the coaches because they weren't going to party all night on Bourbon Street; they wanted to sleep. After the game, we hopped on the bus to the hotel and all filed in and out of their rooms for a quick shower.

But that shower came at a hefty price.

Because he had wheeled us all to the motel to shower, the bus driver couldn't get back behind the wheel for a few extra hours to meet mandatory road safety requirements. Therefore, we would not be boarding or sleeping or going anywhere on our un-air-conditioned bus anytime soon. That shower pit stop left dozens of displaced, clean-but-tired football players scattered along Bourbon Street for longer than we hoped. We did hit the town, but there's only so much partying one can do. We used every available option to wait out our extra time—some people crashed on park benches, some in chairs in hotel lobbies, some on the grass. And we had to do a rotation: I slept on a bench for an hour while someone else stayed awake on guard. Then we would rotate so that everyone could catch some zzz's safely.

We were homeless in New Orleans.

We Were Winning Just by Playing

The New Orleans situation was absurd, and the only way to get through it was to laugh. The funny part was that each and every time it felt like conditions couldn't possibly get worse, bam, they did. Our perks as pro football players slowly slimmed down until even a hotel room was a luxury.

All of the challenges that made us feel as though we were constantly fighting against the world actually brought us together and made us that much closer as a team. Maybe they even contributed to our winningness and dominance. They certainly made us stronger and more determined to be in a place—on the football field—where we simply were not supposed to be. We weren't welcome, but we weren't quitting.

Especially in team sports, challenges can either break you apart or bring you together. Obstacles can be divisive or unifying factors. For us, the harder things got, the more we teamed up. It was us against everybody, week after week. Armed with a healthy sense of humor, we took out our frustrations on each team we played against. Adversity fueled our determination to keep at it.

As the years went by, the conditions deteriorated even more as the margins shrank or the teams got cheaper. We continued to fund-raise our butts off. Short of stealing, we did everything to raise money—unifying to get to that game. As harsh as the conditions were, there's an important point to be made, in fairness to the early pioneers in the league who dared to invest: the owners who started women's football teams weren't multimillionaires who were expanding their portfolio to make more money. The owner of the Dallas Diamonds was Dawn Berndt. She, like the others who owned women's teams back then, simply loved the game of football and wanted to provide the opportunity for women to play. Dawn painted airplanes for a living and started the Dallas Diamonds out of an office in her house. Team owners gave us the foundation, but we all had to carry our weight to keep the dream alive.

COACH JEN:
A DREAM REQUIRES STAMINA AND STRATEGY

- Ignore the money; create a groundswell first.

- While you strive for your chance, you must also take chances.

- You have to push through and keep going through the tough parts.

- Keep your vision clear, even if others don't see it.

- You don't change the game by doing what everybody has always done.

Breakdown or Breakthrough

We knew we were defying the odds by even having and playing in a league of our own. Despite the massive disparity between us and men's professional football, we were all-in. We had this attitude: "We've got to do this." Women were not supposed to be playing football, and yet there we were, getting ready to play for our fourth championship game, with no money to put a team on the field. But we were used to that. That's what we lived with as we battled to battle on the field. Did it piss me off that we had to wash cars in the parking lot for a few bucks? Absolutely. We shouldn't have had to do that—a professional football team hustling like a high school team. With resources so painfully slim it was tough to own the title *pro athlete*.

The end result of a crisis or difficult time is determined by the way you view the situation. When things get difficult, you have to decide: Do you let a situation break you, or do you let it push you to a breakthrough?

Toward the end of a struggle, when things feel as bad as they possibly can, that's when it's breakthrough time. Breakthroughs happen on the heels of what causes 99 percent of people to break down. I truly believe that. In the midst of crisis, you simply don't know what's about to reveal itself, what opportunity is around the corner, what the next step is going to be.

There's a saying: "It's always darkest before the dawn."

When there's nothing but darkness, that's when the breakdown comes. This is your test for everything you tackle: Breakdown or breakthrough? What are you going to do when it seems darkest? Are you going to keep on pushing and pushing, knowing in your heart that there will indeed be one glimmer of light to pull you through, or are you going to let a tough situation break you down?

With no money coming in from football, with no support from the team and management, with terrible conditions, it was tough to hang on to the football dream. I didn't realize how difficult it really was while I played because I was deep in the darkness, scrambling to pay to play. When you're in it, you often just accept what's happening and hope. Plus, we were doing what we loved, what was not supposed to be done. Outsiders might have thought we were losing or that the conditions were so horrible maybe we should have packed it in. Instead, we flipped the script: we were winning simply because we were there.

Some days, playing itself was the breakthrough. Just getting to take the field at all seemed like the highest place we'd go—in our own league, with shabby conditions and benches for beds during away games. It felt as though we were breaking through every day. So breakdown didn't tempt us.

Another saying that I drew strength from during that time: "Your tests become your testimony." All of those things, those tests we faced every game, they held us together. We rallied around them because we were basically playing with house money. We were never supposed to be there in the first place.

LITTLE DID I know as I played, as I struggled through what I thought was my big breakthrough, more breakthroughs were on the way, even bigger ones that I couldn't yet imagine. That's something to remember: just because you've achieved one goal doesn't mean you've topped out. There might be more in store that you haven't even conceived of yet.

Struggles are a part of life regardless of your financial situation, your prestige, your outward signifiers of success. The same goes for football, regardless of where a team landed on the food chain or whether you were a man or a woman, what level you achieved, the threats of injury, the physical demands, the hustle of the game. There's always some struggle at every level. It's more difficult to tackle and overcome struggles when you believe they'll eventually go away. They won't. You need to manage them to survive. You do this by looking for small wins, finding hope and seeing change in little improvements, and by sharing struggles with others. You can either find challenges or find small successes—and your choice is everything.

Struggle builds the foundation for the future, too. It took me a long time to figure out the significance of the darkest-before-dawn mentality. It wasn't until years later when I coached for the Texas Revolution that I was fully able to apply it. When it truly resonated with me, I used it to encourage my players. I had been pushed by all my challenges and struggles, but each time there was a breakthrough at the end. I would tell my guys that the devil gets most active just before sunrise, right when night's the darkest. If they could see just one glimmer of sunshine, their fears and demons have lost forever because they can cling to hope that it's only going to get better and better. That's how life is. That's why we need to wait for the light. It will come. It does every day.

You Never Know What the Breakthrough Is until It Happens

Sticking to a dream is a full-time hustle. It was a slog all those years. What was hardest for the Diamonds was knowing how huge the sport of football is in America. Everybody loved football and rallied around it every Sunday and Monday night. We didn't understand why, if the nation adored the sport, it was so difficult for them to rally around women playing it. We were champions. We were the baddest bitches on the block, and still, we were washing cars for the right to play. That was difficult to swallow. But we did.

Being a female athlete is a full-time hustle. Kind of like life. Because I played under number 47, my joke back then was that I had forty-seven jobs. I had to, to make ends meet. That's true in today's economy, too: it doesn't allow us to focus on one thing. We all have to market ourselves, show our entrepreneurial side, and understand the transactions we're dealing with, whatever our gig is. Your life's to-do list, there's no end to it. You have to get as much done as you can to stay in your game.

Making things even harder, there are still a lot of places the world can't envision women, and therefore doesn't value them there. For one, it's a relatively new societal philosophy that women should be in sports at all. At one point it was generally assumed that women weren't physically capable of participating in sports. It takes a phenomenal occurrence to prove such overgeneralizations wrong. Dana White, president of the Ultimate Fighting Championship, once said that he would never let a female into the UFC. Then along came Ronda Rousey.

The discrepancy in valuing the worth of men and women is particularly pronounced in football. In football, you have guys who make millions of dollars a year, and the max that women make is a dollar per game. Our society talks a lot about the need for equal pay for equal work, and sports is one industry where the pay disparity is pronounced. The truth is that any chance worth chasing takes time to land. It takes a breakthrough like Rousey made in the UFC, and Becky Hammon and Nancy Lieberman made in the NBA. I know it might seem like you'll never get the chance to be that person in your industry. But remember: I didn't start with the goal of making history. I started with *be great and commit.*

COACH JEN: HOW DO YOU KNOW
WHEN TO JUMP AND TAKE A RISK?

A dream is a hustle. Own your side hustle and your dream hustle. Think of the two as complementary. Sustaining your dream hustle requires a baseline of resources so you can develop a plan and position yourself for success. Do not think of pursuing your dream as an all-or-nothing decision. For example, you may need to hold down many different jobs, roles, and responsibilities simultaneously. (Think of my forty-seven jobs: being a female athlete required a full-time hustle. Work by day, play football by night, go to school by late night.) The goal is for your dream hustle to phase out your side hustle or position you to take the opportunity of a lifetime.

Think about it this way: if you start your own business on the side while working full time, at a certain point, the business will be established enough to justify your working it full time. Of course, your success is not guaranteed; there are very few absolute guarantees. However, jobs aren't guaranteed either. The one thing you can control is you—your investment, your work, your passion, your time. Realize that your passions feed every area of your life. Yes, it's true, certain dreams may not become your life or a full-time job. However, that does not mean they are not worth your time or that you should give them up completely. Being passionate about things fuels other areas of your life.

A friend once asked me about how big to dream. I said, "Think about what you might do that will make history." She said, "I'll never make history." I said, "You might."

Take a moment to think of the craziest, wildest dream you have. What's an achievement that might seem too lofty or out of reach? What skills or attributes might you have that would be required to live that dream? Now, think back to what I said earlier: *Constantly evaluate where you are relative to what you are capable of.* Take that lofty dream and list ten skills or attributes someone needs to have to land it. Do any of them look familiar? I bet your list of attributes and the ones needed have crossover. Can you learn or obtain the ones that are missing? Try. You might just make history.

As women who are leading in our fields, who are hustling to make our dreams a reality when we can't see a single role model ahead of us, it's important not only to keep in mind how far we've come but also to create reminders for ourselves of how far we have to go to keep us motivated when the hustle gets to be too much.

For women coaching football, the road to Canton, Ohio, home of the Pro Football Hall of Fame, starts with a plain white coaching T-shirt. Today, my plain white Arizona Cardinals coaching shirt is on display in the HOF, and I couldn't be prouder. Thinking of that shirt brings me back to 2013 when I played for Team USA.

When our Team USA squad played against Team Germany on the Fourth of July, we were required to wear our white practice jerseys. We, the defending gold medalists, were stripped down to basics because, for some reason, we were sent overseas with only one game jersey, and our navy blue was too close to Germany's black, and Germany protested our blue.

We were mad about wearing practice jerseys in the game, but we used our sentiment as fuel. After all, practice jerseys were tougher. Plain football. No names on the back. Just *USA* on the front. Without our names on our backs, we all played for something bigger—the name on the front. We represented our country in a big way. No glitz, no glam; we just got the job done.

My white coaching shirt simply had the Cardinals logo on the front and my name hidden inside; the shirt was cut for a woman. My white shirts—one that symbolized the limited resources we had on Team USA and one I wore as an NFL coach—are symbols of the payoffs of hard work and reminders that we should never stop celebrating how far we've come. NFL players inducted into the Hall of Fame are awarded gold jackets. Hopefully, one day gold jackets will be tailored to a woman's cut as well.

Be the player who is a nightmare opponent and a dream-come-true teammate.

||||||||||||||||||||||||||||||||||||||||||||||||||||||||||||||||||||||||||||

4

What Makes Us Different Makes Us Stronger

> We have to embrace, not fear, our differences. My football family was and continues to be the most diverse and wonderful family. It includes men and women I've played with and against, here and abroad. It includes the people I've coached and been coached by, tackled and been tackled by. My football family is made up of people of every shape, size, creed, color, and sexual orientation. It's made up of people who embody all of those things that can divide our society off the field but that unite us on the field. In football, diversity is strength—a team does not win if we all look the same. It's an example we'd all do well to follow.

ONE OF MY best friends on and off the field is Berta Fitcheard-Brydson. We called ourselves the *one-two punch*. We played together for many years in Dallas and traveled overseas together when we played on Team USA in 2010 and 2013. We were always busting for one another, there for each other through everything. We were like family.

Thanks to our shared football dream, our team was very much like a large family. We were more alike than we were different, despite the fact that we were big, small, black, white, and from all different places in the country, who all did different jobs, with different backgrounds and families. It's fair to say, though, that when people looked at us, likely all they saw were the differences. That's the way our world operates: we automatically see what makes people different. With Berta and me, some people would see a black woman and a white woman.

She and I were always stumbling into some mess and then laughing our way out of it. Our misadventures followed us around the globe. When we landed in Stockholm, Sweden, to represent our country, forty-five-plus women decked out in red, white, and blue basically took over the airport. Berta and I ducked into a store for a sixty-second pit stop to grab a couple of phone cards and drinks. When we came out, somehow our group had vanished. It seemed impossible that every single one of them—coaches and players—were gone. Disappeared. We stood there and looked at each other in our Team USA gear, stunned. We had no idea what to do as we scanned the airport crowds. We had no foreign language skills, no cell service, and no idea where we were supposed to go or how we'd get there. She and I just knew we would stick together, so we sat on a bench. We'd basically punched ourselves out before the event took place on the field.

I looked at Berta sitting next to me. "Hey, B, you better watch out, you might get arrested here for being friends with that little white girl."

This was an inside joke that reminded us just how harshly outsiders could view our friendship and that always eased tense situations. She and I were blind to our differences, but not everybody else was.

Back in 2005, we'd already won one championship, and all the Diamonds were gearing up and determined to win another. We were striking out in a big and dedicated way to do it, too. We held extra speed and agility workouts on nights when we didn't have regular practice. We did workouts on our own and studied film, all while raising money, as always.

One evening, Berta and I had just been to a workout. On the way home, we stopped at the 7-Eleven in Southlake Carroll, Texas, to get gas. It was not a super-remote place, but it was a high-dollar area. Berta drove this big old van, and I pulled up behind her in my sporty silver Audi TT. We both stepped out to fill up our tanks. She rifled through her bag trying to figure out where she had left her wallet. I said, "I got you. Don't worry." We went into the store and paid for both tanks on my card.

Just then, a police officer pulled through the parking lot. I didn't think anything when his cruiser slowed down where we were standing. Berta, however, said, "Welty, see, I don't like that."

"You've never liked cops, B," I joked. "He's just getting a cup of coffee. No big deal."

"All right, all right," she said. "You know me, I'll just kind of watch."

He didn't get out for coffee, though; he just pulled through and left.

We stood there for a little longer, talking. Then that same police car circled back, pulled into the lot again, and did another slow pass, the officer looking right at us.

"Man, Welty," Berta said. "He's shady. I told you I'm right. He's up to something."

"Yeah. That's weird," I admitted. "Even I know that's not right."

We were standing in between the two pumps. Rather than hang around, we quickly said our good-byes, got in our cars, and left. I headed home, immediately forgetting about the police officer when I put the car in first gear, Berta's van's headlights dimming in my rearview.

The next day at practice, Berta pulled me aside. "Welty, you'll never guess what happened. I told you I didn't like that cop, right?"

After we had left the gas station, Berta had headed toward the highway in that blue magic mystery van of hers. The entrance to the on-ramp was a really sharp turn. She flashed her lights to see where she was going. As soon as she did, the cop pulled her over.

She asked the police officer what she had done wrong, and he said he pulled her over for flashing her brights.

"Oh, yeah," she tried to explain. "The highway turn was a little steep, so I wanted to make sure I was okay."

His response: "Do you have any outstanding warrants?"

Taken aback, she mentioned her unpaid parking tickets and started looking for the paperwork in her glove box. The beam of the officer's flashlight panned across the back of the van.

Berta put her hands on the steering wheel. "Sir, can I help you?"

And then the truth was revealed.

"Well, yeah," he said. "I saw you at the gas station talking to the little white girl." He apparently thought Berta had kidnapped that little white girl and stuffed her into the back of the van.

Though Berta told me she wanted to explain to the officer there was no way she ever could have gotten that little white girl into the back of that van—though the white girl looked little, she was in reality extremely jacked—instead she explained who the little white girl was, showed him her championship ring, and described how we were teammates who played football together for the defending champions, the Dallas Diamonds.

In Texas, football is the great equalizer.

"You play for the Diamonds?" as he asked, his demeanor immediately changing. "Do you know Wendy, the kicker?" It turned out Wendy was the officer's cousin.

They agreed that Cousin Wendy was a great kicker with strong legs. He left briefly to check Berta's paperwork, and when he returned from his car, he said that she did in fact have an outstanding warrant, that her lawyer hadn't cleared it up yet, but that she should get on out of there. He agreed to pretend they hadn't met and that he hadn't pulled her over. He just told her to say hi to Wendy from Cousin John.

As she told this story to me, we couldn't contain our laughter, imagining the mental picture this cop had of me, bound and gagged in the back of Berta's van. To the outside world, we were too different to be together. To that officer, something looked wrong, and he relied on outdated stereotypes to make an assumption. He could not possibly imagine that we were teammates and friends because he saw us as fundamentally different. He could not possibly imagine that, as different as we were, we had common ground in our goals, hearts, and spirits. He made a snap judgment that something had to be wrong. He did what too many people do in society, which is judge people on the basis of race or economics or any number of trivial attributes.

What he could not possibly see was that we were family.

This is why football is so powerful: two people play for the Diamonds and Team USA and essentially become family because of our common strengths. On the field, where people come from, what color they are—it simply doesn't matter. On that field, we play beyond the perceptions of the outside world, and that appreciation of each other extends far beyond the sidelines.

For years to follow, that incident provided endless fodder when Berta and the little white girl got into mischief.

Our Shared Football Dream

When I had my tryout with the Mutiny, the newly resurrected NWFL was very much in its infancy. The rebirth of women's football was just getting started. The first iteration of the NWFL began in the seventies with seven teams, but, suffering money problems, it fizzled by the eighties. As the league regained its feet, teams popped up all over the country.

For us to be able to strap up our pads and helmets and play the game that was often referred to as the final frontier for women in sports—the game we couldn't, shouldn't, and wouldn't play— well, it was something special to be a part of that. We knew we were doing something important for women. We were making history. The last thing we worried about were the things that made us different. Women before us who worked to launch the sport through to the Diamonds team, all of us, we didn't care about trivial differences. Our drive was the same. Each individual effort was put toward our singular team goal.

Our most significant common thread was that we shared the same football dream, even though we had been told for years that it was not a legitimate dream to have. We held out for so long to play, when we finally got the chance, we formed an intensely close family. Off the field, if a player needed help, we were there for each other, and on the field, it was the same thing. Individually, we were all flawed humans, but collectively, we were pretty darn near perfect.

Our determination for what we were doing and what drove us—this intense love of football—made us different from most other people. We were standouts. Deep in our hearts, we believed that, eventually, women's football would hold a significant place in this country. That our efforts on and off the field were in fact changing the game. There was a greater calling, a bigger picture that we played for. We were fascinated by the game and knew that playing at all was winning.

How I see it: Our commonality made us strong. Our differences made us stronger. When I made the team, it was a heaven-defying moment. My unlikely difference was my small size, but I found my place in the most unlikely of places. Why? Because someone saw something in me. Rather than make that snap she's-too-small decision, the coaches let me prove myself, they gave me a chance to show how my difference could be a strength. That understanding, that diversity of strength, was critical to the team and made it possible for me to be judged on my athletic merits alone.

As a rookie, I was pretty much relegated to the kickoff team, so I figured if I was going to be on kickoff team, then I was going to maximize my impact by leading the team in tackles. Not only did I lead through my statistics but also I led in attitude—an attitude I had acquired over a lifetime of being told I was too small. I was a bit of a firecracker. I instigated others, pushing them to step up and be competitive on special teams as well. When I first got on the field for kickoffs, other players dreaded that particular special team. We were the backups and the rookies. But soon, we developed into a squad that sent a message and set the tone for the game. Eventually, we sent such a powerful message on kickoff, players actually competed to join in the squad.

Today, embracing the mentality that a perceived difference or weakness can actually turn into a strength is crucially important, though it's overlooked and underrated. Individually, everyone on our team faced some sort of bias in her personal life. And as a group, as women who wanted to break through, just wanting to play football forced us to face biases. To many people, our sex made us unfit to play. They didn't see it as acceptable or doable; football, for some, was still a thing that women can't do. On top of that, we had me, this tiny player. We also had women who looked skinny and women who came from backgrounds that didn't fit a stereotypical "football" narrative. It was all the more ironic, then, that we found our place in football.

But it's a beautiful irony and encapsulates in its purist form the notion that we can't judge, we can't set limits, we must dismiss preconceived notions, and we must let people in, even when we don't expect them to fit.

COACH JEN: DIVERSITY IS STRENGTH

That officer who pulled Berta over did what too many people do: he judged her on the basis of preconceived ideas; judgment might be based on race, appearances of class, or other surface stuff. And yet, diversity is a strength because it makes us see the bigger picture, imagine beyond the lines of race and economics and gender, and accomplish more as a result. Lack of diversity—or an inability to embrace it—constrains us all. It makes us think small, not play big. When we can accept diversity, we grow bigger than our own limitations. When we embrace differences, we accomplish things we might not have been able to do by ourselves.

In football, finding each player's special skills is an essential aspect of fielding a winning team. Can you catch the ball, yes or no? If you can't catch, you're not a receiver. We might still have a place for you, but receiver is not it. If you are big and strong and protective, you probably will be on the O-line. If you're big and strong and fast and aggressive, you'll probably be on the D-line. If you read and react, you'll probably be on defense. If you're more calculating and tactical, you'll probably be on offense.

As many have often said, football is the ultimate meritocracy. In football, all of these judgments are objective assessments based on skills. Though, sure, these types of evaluations point to our differences, but superficial ones. They are fact-based, performance-based assessments. You can see these skills play out in real time. And these are not assessments of a person's intrinsic attributes that stem from a certain ethnicity or race or socioeconomic status or even a college degree. They come from straight-out performance.

Sadly, off the field the differences in people oftentimes terrify others. Many fail to take the time to really get to know what part or aspect of a person is great—where she came from, what she is made of. Progress has been made, but we have a long way to go. The more we can realize that what makes someone different makes her special, the better off and more efficient and strong our society and our workplaces will be.

COACH JEN: GET TO KNOW YOUR PEOPLE

Ignore what is on the outside and get to know what's on the inside of a person, especially if you're putting together a team. Ask yourself,

- What makes her different?
- What motivates her?
- Why is she great?
- What does she love?
- In what situation will she shine?

Tap into people as individuals to get to know them. See beyond outside attributes, and get to the core of who each person is beyond what they do.

The Cardinals Embraced What
Made Me Different

After I joined the Cardinals, Bruce Arians often repeated why he pursued me to be one of his coaches: because I brought a different perspective to the staff. After watching me at work, he recognized it was my ability to see each player's differences that made me good at what I did; I tapped into the guys as individuals.

During training camp, before the preseason games had begun, Markus Golden, one of the Cardinals' linebackers, was having a rough practice. Markus, an outside linebacker, was tasked with keeping outside contain: to hold the edge and let no player outside of him while bringing pressure and rushing the quarterback. Though I was assigned to work with the inside linebackers at training camp, I played outside most of my career, so I knew the position.

For defense, the quickest route to the bench is touching your own quarterback. It is very important to avoid risk of injury and it's why quarterbacks wear red jerseys—red means stop. Well, on this particular play, Markus did not touch the QB, but he came close, and the way he avoided the QB was a risky move. Essentially, when coming off the edge, to avoid contact, a linebacker can either run behind the quarterback, which would maintain outside contain, or run underneath him. That day, Markus avoided the quarterback by running underneath him, and it was bad for two reasons. Number one, it raised the risk of running into the quarterback because of the limited space between the QB and the offensive line. Two, it yielded a bad habit. The aiming point for the quarterback is the up-field shoulder, so a good, mobile QB like Cam Newton or Aaron Rodgers cannot roll outside of the pocket and break contain.

After that move, Markus was called out. It's part of the game of football to get yelled at, but some days it hits hard, especially when you get reamed more than once in a day and especially when you are a rookie. Defense gets yelled at all the time. I knew from experience that the frequency doesn't make it easy. And I knew from watching Markus that he might take it personally.

After practice, back at the hotel, I ran into Markus in the hallway outside of the meeting room, so I took him aside for a minute.

Markus towered over me. "Markus, do you realize why we were so hard on you today?"

"No, Coach," he said. "I don't."

"Because you've got *it*. We can see it in you. When we tell you something, it's not necessarily that you did something wrong, but it's definitely because it could be that much more right. As coaches, the greatest gift that we can give you is to help you get better. You never have to worry when we are coaching you up, because that means we see potential. Worry when we don't coach you, because then we have given up."

He looked at me for a moment. "I've never really thought about it that way, Coach."

"You know what, Markus? When I was playing, I didn't think about it that way either. I was *that* player: I was hardheaded. I took coaching personally, and I didn't always respond well."

I wished that when I was a player somebody had told me what I was telling him: that the greatest gift a coach can give a player is to make him or her better. And when a coach is calling a player out or pointing out flaws, though it feels rough, it's because coaches see potential.

He smiled. I could tell by the way he looked that some weight had been lifted from him, that what I said made an impact. His reaction was a great signal that I was doing my job as coach.

Bruce saw us talking and came over to follow up with Markus. I attempted to excuse myself, assuming he wanted a private talk with his player, but Coach stopped me. "No, Coach, stay." So I did.

He, too, reviewed keeping outside contain and avoiding the quarterback with Markus. And then when Markus left, Bruce said to me, "You had 100 percent of Markus's attention, he was really listening to you. What were you talking about when I walked up?"

"Well," I said, "on the football side, pretty much what you just said. But I also told him that we were on him in part because he had *it*. We were coaching him to make him better. And that he never had to worry as long as we were coaching him up and were able to see where he could improve. We saw potential. The only time he had to worry was when we got quiet."

"Yup, that's when players get cut. Good work, Coach."

Bruce and I saw the situation the same way, and he confirmed my instincts.

As a player, I had been in Markus's cleats many times. So, on that day, as a coach, I could explain what he needed to do differently as a player; as a person, I could give him the insight I wished I'd had when I was a player. To put it simply, in Bruce's words, I "read his eyes" instead of treating him like a robotic player, like someone who wouldn't take the coaching personally—I looked close enough to see what emotional reaction was showing in his eyes, and I adjusted my coaching accordingly.

BRUCE ARIANS: IN HIS OWN WORDS

When you look at someone's eyes and they're talking to you, you see what you need to find out. You see passion. You see deception. You see fear. You see knowledge. All of these things come out in a person's eyes when they're speaking to you. And if a person is not looking straight into your eyes when they're talking to you about something they're passionate about, or that you think they're passionate about, then they're not passionate. Or they don't know what they're actually talking about. A long, long time ago, as a bartender, I learned to read eyes. When Jen was dealing with me, she was straightforward and looked me dead in the eye with conviction. And that's when I knew that she knew she could teach.

COACH JEN: READ PEOPLE'S EYES

Bruce always told me that I did a great job reading players' eyes. That means

- Building a personal connection based on important individual differences

- Seeing past preconceived notions and generalities to form a genuine relationship

- Reading the individual and his or her responses to situations, *and* believing what you read in their eyes—even if it's going to be tough to deal with

- Tapping into each person's differences in a way that they can respond to. Everyone reacts to different stimuli, and

→

what one person needs and answers to will be different from that of another.

- Investing conversations with personal insight, but putting the other person's feelings and needs at the forefront of the conversation

- Being empathetic and relating to someone else's situation, then engaging based on trust and understanding

- Developing a coach-athlete (or mentor-mentee) relationship founded in mutual trust and respect while also being flexible in your approach and being willing to be coached yourself

- Remembering that some days your team, your family, your friends—they need high fives; other days, they need a kick in the butt

One of the beautiful things about football is the diversity required to make a team successful. Talents, skill sets, and personalities vary significantly from player to player and position to position. When we're in street clothes, most people would not look at us and identify us as a group. When we're in street clothes, our individual differences make us appear separate. However, when we put on our uniforms, the individual differences take on a greater purpose. A team relies on each player's completing an individual job in order for plays to be successful. It is beautiful, really.

If all the players on a team were built the same way and had the same talents, we would get killed. Football just doesn't work if all eleven people are identical, or if the coaches treat every player alike. The best coaches see what individual players need, then make sometimes subtle and sometimes major adjustments to give it to them. Think about it: Should somebody play receiver if they can't catch? Or play linebacker if they can't tackle? But if you have a linebacker with speed, heart, great hands, and skill who can't tackle, maybe you take the time to identify those strengths and that difference, and you discover that person might be a fantastic running back. Someone with great instinct and aggression and no hands might better serve the team playing defense. That's the beauty of football—there's room for all sorts of skills and perspectives.

Is it so different in your industry? Would you want to be on a staff of people who were all the same? Of course not. What kind of a work division would you have if everyone were great with numbers but not with people? But go further than that—think about how you can read the eyes of your colleagues, your students, your family members, even. What do they need, particularly from you, so that you can all work together to reach for your greatest potentials?

Everybody gets hit. When you do, you get back up and do it with attitude.

||||||||||||||||||||||||||||||||||||||||||||||||||||||||||||||||||||||||||||

5

Getting Back Up

You are never truly powerless. Your power source is internal. Don't ever give that away. If you are not in control of a situation, then you need to examine the dynamics and evaluate whether you want and need to be in it. Once you've decided, focus on what you can control, and work toward taking small steps—I promise you, they will build into big changes.

IN OUR SOCIETY, rings are a sign of commitment, and a sign of success. Some rings, like championship rings, cannot be bought; they can only be won. A clear sign of my true love was when I replaced my engagement ring on my finger with my first championship ring (a women's football Super Bowl ring). I used to say with a laugh that I was married to football, which might have been foreshadowing, considering what happened with my ex. After all, I stayed with the game through all the ups and downs, the wins and losses, joys and tears, for better or worse, and at times it felt like only death could keep us apart.

Asking yourself what you love is a great first step toward your greatness. But examining your commitment—asking, What am

I committed to? What sparks my passion and willingness to live each moment as if it were my last?—can be even more illuminating. Making a commitment is the less-recognized but just as important second step in achieving real fulfillment. Find something you love *and* commit to it. Carefully consider which relationships and which activities pull you through, which ones will give you long-term inspiration. For the long haul, your commitment will be what inspires you the most, what pushes you forward. In evaluating what's worthy of your love and commitment, you might just find your greatness.

AT THE HEIGHT of my football career in 2008, from the outside my life looked normal—enviable, in fact. Nobody would have suspected the apple cart had been tipped. But, in fact, in January of that year, I was homeless, living out of my little Audi TT. My life had been characterized by many professional accomplishments but also some major personal failures.

My car was a silver hard top with black leather seats and a tiny backseat, too. The backseat remained down to provide a meticulously organized extended truck. I could easily grab what I needed from my mobile home base. I could put the front seat down on that little sports car and sleep. It might have been different for a six-foot-tall guy, but for me, at five-foot-two, it was perfect. It was the ultimate traveling suitcase. I would occasionally hit up friends for a couch to crash on, but I was generally very quiet about my situation. I didn't want pity and I didn't want anyone to worry. My parents didn't know. My employer didn't know. My teammates certainly didn't know.

I showered at the gym where I worked as a trainer. I worked all day. At the end of each day, I went to football practice. Then I went *home*. Just like everyone else. Only my home was my car.

It should have been the worst time of my life. But it was the absolute opposite. Aside from a small storage unit, that car and its contents were the only things I owned—all 100 percent mine, paid for in full. That thrilled me. See, I had finally escaped the grips of a relationship that for me felt destructive and emotionally abusive. Despite the gravity of my financial situation, outside of the time I spent playing football, for the first time in many, many years, I felt free.

The reality was that since I had moved to Dallas, my relationship with my then-boyfriend had steadily deteriorated. When I stepped out onto the football field, I left everything else in my life behind. It was the one and only place in my world that I could really be present and absorb the moment while tuning out the rest of the noise. All of life's issues, distractions, problems, insecurities—football eclipsed them all. Nothing existed on the field but football. There, I was magic. We all played with that same level of engagement even while experiencing struggle and sacrifice just to have our chance to do so. Football saved me.

But through all of those years, though I shared my football dream with my football family and my friends, I never shared the depths of the problems I was facing at home. In fact, until the writing of this book, I never really told many people. I wasn't just trying to save them from worrying about me. I was also too embarrassed, too afraid of being vulnerable and showing weakness to share it. I didn't want people to focus on what was bad in my life because I was doing so many good things.

Being homeless should have been my rock-bottom moment. Instead, it was one of the greatest periods in my life. Living out of my car gave me the strength to know I could do just about anything. It fueled me in an unimaginable way. And though it was certainly a challenging existence, it honed a sharp knowingness inside of me that I could do anything with my life. I would later draw upon that certainty on my path to making history.

WHEN I WAS twenty-six, I moved across the country from Massachusetts to Dallas, Texas, with that boyfriend. By that point, playing for the Mutiny had broken my heart and broken me financially. I had put in a ton of sweat equity in addition to an enormous investment of my own money, maxing out my credit cards to support the team and do things like buy team uniforms. But I lost my investment when circumstances changed.

I had been dating my boyfriend for less than a year, but when he asked me to move, I did. I was so off balance professionally that I let him swoop in and play hero. He loved that. I put my trust in him because I had lost faith in myself. I agreed to move across the country not because I was in love but because I figured I had just about nothing left to lose. I told him I would move as long as there was a football team where we were going. I couldn't lose that.

So, I left behind all that I knew and all my support on the East Coast. I was following my love. But it wasn't my love of the boy, it was my love of the game and my promise to follow that no matter where it took me.

Before him, I had dated only tall guys. He was shorter—just five-ten, muscularly built, and very much Mister Corporate Guy. When I met him I thought he was the nicest man on the face of the earth, and I used that as justification because he was not my type. Things between us were great at first, and then they just weren't. There were many reasons, but it seemed like the more successful I got, and the more engaged and excited I grew about my football potential—eventually joining that amazing Diamonds team—the worse our relationship got. He went from being my hero to my villain.

Once we got to Dallas, within a blink, we were engaged. That proposal in and of itself should have been my clue to get out. We were at a seafood restaurant in Dallas. I don't remember if he got down on his knee or not, I just remember the ring. Many women have this heart-skips-a-beat moment when they see an engagement ring. I didn't. It mostly felt wrong. It was wrong: this commercial-looking bright yellow-gold ring. Though it fit on my finger, it didn't fit me.

The situation was forced, and just as he was about to ask the question to go with the ring, I stopped him. "Have you called my dad to ask permission?"

"No," he said.

It was so important to me, I made him call—as in, pull out his phone and call from the restaurant—before he continued with the proposal. He completed the call quickly and then said, "Will you marry me?"

"Yes," I said, but as I looked down at that ring, I immediately thought, *Has this guy ever met me? Does he even know me?* The ring had a big, round diamond. It wasn't something I would have chosen, or worn, and any single human on earth who knew me would have known that. The ring did not belong on my finger.

Without a lot of discussion, I was suddenly invested in a life I wasn't overly enthusiastic about. It was a whirlwind, and I got wrapped up in it. We then very quickly bought a house together and my name was on the deed, so there was this illusion of security. We even got dogs together. Our lives were quickly entwined.

I had built a busy Texas life, with a job at a gym as a trainer, making the cut for the Diamonds, and getting close to finishing my master's degree in sport psychology by taking a class or two at a time. As I chased my dreams, I gave up my full-time job because he did very well financially. So while I played football and went to school, I also slowly and somewhat blindly grew dependent on him. Simultaneously and almost without noticing, with all that was happening in my life, I was quietly becoming isolated, and my commitment to him grew based on all of our new ties and things that we owned together. But I was unknowingly being separated from my comfort, my people, and my independence.

And then, the fighting began. Maybe it had always been there and I hadn't noticed. He would get jealous over even the simplest of things, and that jealousy would lead to a fight. To me he was destructive and chaotic. Everything was urgent, like a fire. I walked on eggshells, never knowing exactly what would set him off. Most of our fights were over football—my playing, my not being there for him because I was away at practice, and so on. That one thing I loved somehow threatened him terribly. What he initially loved about me became the thing he hated. I was damn good on the football field, and he couldn't control that, though he certainly seemed to resent it.

I never quite knew how bad it would get, and although I knew the relationship was off the mark, I didn't make a move to leave. Over the years, the anger escalated.

"Why are you doing this football thing?" he said one evening at home while sipping his pink wine. He loved pink wine. "There's no future in it."

I shrugged off the comment. I'd grown used to them, but he kept picking at me. And he picked at me with increasing frequency, it seemed.

The fighting became a regular occurrence. It became clear that nothing I did was ever right or good enough. Still, it was strange. He never laid a finger on me. But I somehow always felt terrified that at any second he could. He was never physically violent with me, but I was increasingly afraid that would change. The arguments escalated; I fought back a little more each time. The walls in our house looked terrible for all the holes he had punched in them. Looking back, it was the typical abuse dynamic. The guy was the nicest person you'd ever meet, and then he wasn't. I stayed longer than I should have, but we had become so tied together. Many nights, I cried myself to sleep.

Broke Me Down without My Even Knowing It

Eventually, he would do anything to demean me. "It's a good thing you're pretty because you have nothing else going for you," he would say. I had championship rings, football, and two degrees. Coming out of his mouth in that way, *pretty* became an ugly and demeaning word. He called me vain when I worked out even though working out was success-driven for me, a key component of being a professional athlete and actually my source of income. He would mock my degrees, saying they were a waste of money because, after all, he was a college dropout with "an MBA in real life" who made more money than his fiancée with a master's degree.

Working out was vain, football was useless, degrees were a waste of money, and pretty was all I had going for me. He diminished everything good in my life. I think he must have wanted me to feel weak. Not strong. I think he must have wanted me to feel lucky to have him because nobody else would want me. He kicked my feet out from under me—and *just pretty* was his way. I didn't want to see myself that way after hearing that from him. Sometimes I let that sort of thing in; most days I worked to purge it from my system on the football field. But it was a long time before I undid the impact of that it's-a-good-thing-you're-pretty fight. Here's how I did it, albeit years later:

After playing women's pro football for many seasons, I popped by an open tryout for the Dallas Desire, a team starting in the lingerie league. I went to their tryout with some serious attitude, assuming I'd show these pretty girls a thing or two about playing football. Let me be clear: talk about underestimated performers. Sure, these girls were beautiful, many of them models, but a good number of them were also exceptional athletes. They won me over and, in a sense, laid the groundwork for me to open my mind about how a person can be more than one thing. It took me a long time to accept the *and* in myself. I ultimately ended up coaching the team.

Through the Desire, I met a photographer named Rashard Dabney. He asked if I'd let him photograph me. He showed me a picture of me he had taken at a tryout. I looked full of attitude wearing a Superman T-shirt. It didn't feel like me. But he was right. It was beautiful.

"I want to do a photo shoot with you," he said. "I want you to model."

"You're crazy. I'm not one of those girls. I'm not pretty like a model," I said.

"Trust me," he said. "You photograph beautifully. But you're stuck on what a model looks like. You're muscular and strong and people need to see that."

He convinced me. I did the photo shoot. And when I first saw the pictures I didn't even recognize myself. I remember looking at the images in shock. And I remember Rashard's saying, "This is you. I don't understand why you don't see this."

I was torn about making them public, wondering whether I could be the person I wanted to be—an expert in psychology, a tough football player, and a mentor—and at the same time a model? One who did feminine photo shoots? I struggled with it because the labels were so deeply ingrained in my head. A part of me was still afraid to be seen as "just pretty." I still felt like considering myself pretty could be a weapon used against me.

Ultimately, when I got square with the idea, it was one of the coolest feelings of my life. I had ignored that side of me for years. Suddenly, those irrational reactions to being pretty subsided. I had let my ex mess with my head about my looks, but he didn't have that power anymore.

Those photos gave me a new sense of self. I felt strong *and* pretty *and* smart, and I was *still* a tough football player. I had to be tough on the field to survive, but it took someone else's seeing me objectively to help me adjust my thinking about being an *and,* not an *or.* I was tough. And I was pretty. And I was smart. As women, we forget that sometimes. I know I did.

And then, it finally hit me: there's no such thing—there shouldn't be, anyway—as this notion of traditional beauty. Badass is beautiful. Strong is an acceptable quality in a woman in any scenario. We can be badass and beautiful simultaneously. There's no compromise. There's no need to be one thing or another. Combining all of those things makes us special.

We did another photo shoot later and Rashad produced the pictures I became best known for. They were inspired by the character and persona I had created for myself on the field—the Grrridiron Girl. She was tough as nails, but definitely a girl. And sexy in her strength. No one could ever tell her she was *just* pretty. Beauty, brains, and a beast on the football field, the Grrridiron Girl owned her personal power. And, finally, she owned it off the field, too. More on her later.

Salvation in Plaster

Back to my ex: eventually, I stopped letting friends come to my house because of the holes in the walls. But those holes ended up pointing me to my salvation.

To complete my doctorate, I needed to choose a six-week period during which I could write my comprehensive exam. It was a sixty-page, four-question essay exam. I couldn't miss the deadline by even one minute or I failed, and the essay couldn't be longer than sixty pages on the button or I failed. I had worked on this degree for years. I put a lot of heart into finishing. I decided that the last day of my six weeks, the day I'd finish, would be my thirtieth birthday. In advance I tackled every project that might distract me during those six weeks—paid bills, cleaned the house, you name it. It was in the beginning of football season and I was loving it, so that was about to heap my plate pretty high, too.

My ex worked out of an office with peach painted walls, the largest room in the house, and absolutely the prime real estate. I had loved that color when I painted the room, but eventually it felt as rotten as our relationship. It made me feel angry every time I walked into that room. I used to think, *He looks like the devil behind his desk.* I didn't want to spend my six weeks in that room. That office was his and his alone. I hadn't established my own office or even my own desk in the house. So I claimed a guest bedroom that had never housed any guests as my sanctuary.

I wanted to paint the room blue. In addition to carving out an office, I decided to address the rest of the house as well. Fueled by the impending start of my six weeks, I figured I'd spackle over all the holes in the walls. He expressed his anger with his fists, not on me, but on the walls of our life together. During one fight, tears flowed down my face and I fought to move air into my lungs as I watched him slam through the sheetrock. I watched the devastation, paralyzed, a helpless bystander in the destruction of our house. When he stopped, I realized our lives were riddled with holes of destruction—the mangled walls were concrete proof of that.

I wanted a clear head for my six-week run. I wanted the holes and what they reminded me of gone. I started patching holes in the middle of the large wall but quickly realized that just spackling over them wouldn't fix them because the patches didn't blend with the rest of the wall. I would have to cover the entire wall. So I bought a book on texturing walls and discovered a wonderful technique, Venetian plaster.

One day early in the morning, I started plastering. By late afternoon, I had not stopped.

And he was still sleeping away on the couch in a dirty, white, pit-stained T-shirt, unshaven, utterly disgusting. Once he finally woke up, he wandered into the kitchen where I had been relentlessly plastering.

There I was, looking a mess, still working, and covered in plaster. He just looked at me with his hand down the front of his shorts and said, "Wanna have sex?" I threw up a little in my mouth and through the bile I said, "You want to have a shower?" He said, "I was just kidding." But I wasn't kidding. I was serious. In that moment I knew: *I'm never having sex with this man ever again.* I was so repulsed. I couldn't believe he was even a part of my life.

I thought, *I'm fixing everything. I'm done with this. Everything. I'm changing my life.*

That one day of work grew into many days, and I wound up Venetian-plastering multiple rooms in the house. I plastered over my pain and, in a sense, I saved myself in the process. Venetian plaster is one of the best substances on the face of the earth. Even the ugliest, most distorted surface can be transformed into a masterpiece. By plastering those walls, I learned no holes were too deep, no damage too profound to be beyond repair. Once I'd finished plastering, I knew in my heart that, eventually, I'd be able to fix my life as well.

Of course, I didn't get to fix my life until everything that could go wrong did go wrong and stood in the way of my finishing my degree.

My computer crashed and my ex, an IT expert, "fixed it." That became a pattern. It inexplicably crashed over and over, and I waited for him to fix it. My valuable time ticked away, and my deadline approached quickly. It seemed to me that he relished the control he had over me.

Then, down to the wire, the night before my birthday, I realized I was over the sixty-page max. It was imperative I answer with exactly sixty pages. I started reformatting, rewriting, and reworking. After having read it over and over so many times, I was bleary-eyed. My future hung in the balance of these words.

He entered my little blue sanctuary. "Do you need some help?" This was a rare nice gesture on his part. It was what I had been craving. He was actually stepping up to help. It felt too good to be true. I wasn't sure whether he was sincere, but I also wasn't sure what would happen if I said no.

I said yes. "Would you do a quick proofread so I have an extra set of eyeballs?"

He agreed, with stipulations. Typical.

Three hours later, I walked downstairs to hear what he had to say about my work only to find that he was lying on the couch asleep. With all my pages on his chest. He had not even folded over the first page. That showed me everything I needed to know. My future was on the line, and he was sleeping soundly.

I worked through the night and submitted the paper online the next morning. But there was a technical glitch on the submission site and my official submission was rejected. When I called to ensure my document had been received, I learned my fiancé had not turned in the paperwork to pay for my semester. So, the course I had spent so much time working at had not even been paid for. My work might not count and I might have to start from scratch another semester.

After weeks of intense work and no sleep, I realized my coursework might not count toward my degree or I'd fail for not turning it in on time. If I failed my comprehensive exams, all of the work I had done to earn my PhD would have been for nothing. My dream of becoming Dr. Jen would have been a total fail.

I collapsed on the floor of my blue office in sheer frustration. I curled up in a ball on the floor and fell asleep as my dogs kissed away the salty tears. Happy birthday to me.

I had to wait one long week and suffer through a lot of tears to find out whether I would graduate. Thankfully, the school worked with me on the technical and financial challenges. My comprehensive exams were over, but so was my relationship. I knew I was leaving. I just didn't yet know how.

COACH JEN: TYPICAL ABUSE DYNAMIC

Remember that abuse comes in many forms—physical, but also emotional. If you are being manipulated with threats, or degraded and put down, that's abuse. My ex never hit me. However, he would get very mad, which caused me to fear him. He manipulated me with actions that made me feel afraid, like punching a wall close to my head.

Abusive behavior can enter the relationship gradually, which is why many victims don't recognize it. Women who are abused often don't realize the dynamics, because abuse doesn't start on day one. It's a slow burn. You don't go on a first date with someone, get assaulted, then fall in love. Of course not, because you would promptly call the police and cut it off before the end of the date. At first, everything

→

> seems great. Perfect. But slowly, over time, that changes. Ties are established, then dependence. My ex encouraged me to quit working so I could focus on school. That sounded generous. But once I did, he made it clear that he controlled the money and, therefore, me. I was stuck. He had control. Over the years, bit by bit, he discouraged my relationships with friends from growing and maintained distance from my family. I was growing isolated and I didn't even realize it was happening. Suddenly, it seemed, like in most of these types of relationships, I had an octopus wrapped around me. Even if I sliced off one tentacle, seven more still entangled me.

Sunlight and Peace

I went home to Florida for Christmas. My fiancé was supposed to join me, but he was a no-show. The distance was good for my sanity, but I had no good answers to my family's questions about his absence.

Two days before the holiday, my parents and I were out on a boat. Wearing a pink and green bikini, I sat on the front of the boat, catching sun, taking in the glaring streaks of orange and pink spiking across the sky as the sun set in the water. Suddenly, the strangest thing happened. An immense and all-consuming feeling of peace washed over me. Despite the stress of not hearing from my fiancé for days, I felt happier in that moment than I had in a long time. I had been so consumed by his chaos that I hadn't felt peace in so long. The feeling was overwhelming, but in a good way.

My peace was shattered when our boat came back into cell range. He hadn't responded to any of my calls or texts, so I texted him, *Are you alive?* He responded immediately, *I am, not that you care.* Then he proceeded to list all the things about me that made him sick . . . In response to his long list, I simply typed, *I don't want to make you sick anymore. Let's not be together ever again.*

He must have panicked, responding, *No, that's not what I meant.* But it was too late. I texted back, *No. I'm going to give you your freedom. We're done.*

It was over. I didn't say anything to my parents right away. I was in shock. But later, out on the back porch, my dad noticed something was wrong.

"Are you all right?" he asked.

"I think so, Daddy," I said. "I just broke up with my fiancé via text message."

With wonderful calm, he said, "Okay, here's what I am going to do. I'm going to go inside and make you a drink. Then, I'm bringing it out here, and you are going to drink it. When you're done, I'm going to refill your glass. And then, if you want to talk to me about it, cool. If you don't, that's okay, too." He ruffled my hair like he used to when I was a kid.

My pops went inside and made two vodka grapefruits. He came out, put one on the table, and did not say a word. He walked away and left me alone with my thoughts. I should have been upset or maybe crying. I had been engaged to this guy for so long. But I wasn't sad at all. I was okay. I knew it was over. But I was okay.

My only regret: breaking up with him while I was away. This gave him time to do some financial destruction. I never imagined he would do the things he did, and when I finally got back to Dallas it took me a while to discover the extent of his malice.

I did my best to stay away from the house while I figured how to move out. My ex quickly changed the locks, and I learned after a couple of visits that he had moved a new girlfriend into our house and hid her in our bedroom (behind a locked door!) each time I went there. I caught her once and that was it. I was out. My car was my new home. And I couldn't have been happier.

Many times he had promised that if I ever left, he would do everything in his power to ruin my life. What he didn't know: he wasn't that powerful. He had watched me tackle the biggest and baddest women in football and then pop back up and do it again with attitude. He should have known he couldn't break me.

Once I made up my mind that I was done, even though it meant living out of my car, I never once considered going back. He had used up his second chances. Despite the difficulties that ensued, it was one of the best moves of my life. I was thrilled to have escaped.

COACH JEN: CHECK THE CHARACTER OF THE CHARACTERS IN YOUR LIFE

- Trust your gut—if something seems off with someone, it likely is.

- Watch how they act and behave. Is it consistent or erratic?

- How do they treat other people?

- What are their friends like?

- When you ask tough questions, do they yell as a defense mechanism or power play?

- Do they get sensitive when you ask personal questions?

- Look at people you share your life with from a holistic perspective. Introduce them to your family and friends, and solicit feedback. Remember that the people who love you will want you to live up to your potential, not hold you back.

- Don't worry how far or deep in you are. Get out when you know it is wrong.

The Value of Commitment

Moving into that car was pure freedom. When I left him, I was broke, but I was far from broken. His grip on me—the one that I felt closing around my throat—was finally gone. I was free. I was ecstatic. The house we shared was beautiful and ugly at the same time. It was a gilded cage. It might have been pretty on the outside, but it was still a cage.

But I still had football. It was then that I realized how important my commitment to the game was to my well-being. Being on that field breathed life into me every day. And having a burden in my life lifted made me play even better. Surviving that relationship taught me the importance of carefully considering what in life is worthy of my commitment and to use what I naturally committed to as signs of my purpose. Looking back, it's so clear to me that the two constants in my life—my studies and my football—were my passions, the things I could pour myself into.

Be Vulnerable

It might have been a mistake to hide what I was going through from those closest to me. Through all of those ups and downs, I didn't want to show my vulnerability to my teammates or my friends. Knowing what I know now and being able to reflect, I could have opened up. I used to think that my strength was never admitting any weakness. Today, I realize that true strength, as truly strong people will tell you, comes from knowing weakness—knowing where you are great and where you are vulnerable.

When I think back on those times, I'm truly conflicted: How could I have been so strong and so powerful on the field and such a total wreck in the rest of my life? The sad thing is that I could have told so many people about my struggles. I could have told my parents—they're amazingly supportive. My football family was, too.

I should have told them. I suppose some of them had their suspicions. But I didn't want them to see me as less than that player I was on the field.

This is something a lot of athletes do, and maybe a lot of women who are living through adversity, too. We are taught never to admit fear, never to admit weakness, because that could diminish what we're doing. You can never let the opponent see you crack, right? And you'd never want your teammates to doubt that you have their back, that you have your shit together, and that you are a great teammate. And yet, inside every working person and every player, even the baddest linebacker in the game, is a real and live person with real-life problems.

In the game of life, nobody is perfect. Trust that those around you know that and don't expect perfection. Remember that sometimes, too, our weaknesses can actually breed and inspire our strengths.

The true impression a player makes is not captured in the plays. Those moments in between the plays can be just as powerful.

|||||||||||||||||||||||||||||||||||||||||||||||||||||||||||||||||||||||||||||||||||||

6

Success Isn't Just Talent, It's Fortitude

Let me be clear: I was not the best woman who ever played football, without a doubt. There were people who were bigger, faster, stronger. I played with, against, and among them for years. But it was my fortitude—keeping going instead of breaking down—that helped me break through. Every step in my journey, every game, every win, and every letdown, ultimately set the stage for me to make it to an unimaginable destination.

I CAN MARK the actual defining moment when I went from playing football to being a football player. Hitting rock bottom actually helped bounce me up to that new status. It made my drive to fight that much greater. It made the struggle more real but also gave me more desire to overcome it. And that new status on the field was bigger than football. It represented much more.

The year I moved into my car, the Dallas Diamonds made the championship game for the fourth time, and we were to play in Chicago against the Chicago Force. The teams had never played each other before, so it was a big game. Chicago was statistically favored to win, plus we were the away team, and we were broke. Our playoff season had been expensive. We had had to fly to Seattle—last minute, which meant high airline pricing—to play so we could even make it to Chicago.

Here we were, with three championships under our belt—an amazing team by men's or women's football standards—and still there were no major sponsors to get us to the big game. Instead of focusing on physically and mentally preparing to play, we had to scramble in every way possible to pay for our trip there. Getting fifty-plus women on a plane and in hotel rooms in a major city was costly. We hit up friends, we solicited donations, we tracked down alumni players, and we used our own money to get the funding together. It was the ultimate hustle just to get to Chicago, but we did it. We would not be denied.

Right before we officially took the field that day, I got a special call from Drew Pearson, former Dallas Cowboy, NFL legend, but mostly my friend. He had always looked out for me. He knew that it had been a tough year for me.

"It's Eight-Eight. Play the game of your life tonight, Four-Seven," he said.

In the face of the hostile home crowd, Eighty-Eight knew just how to fuel my fire. I smiled. Damn right it was *The Game of My Life*.

The 2008 Chicago Force versus Dallas Diamonds championship meeting was one of those epic games you live your entire career to play. The stadium was sold out, and the fences were lined with fans trying to get in. The entire crowd was decked out in Force red and black, except one sliver of Diamonds Purple that cut through the center of their fans: the underdogs coming in to take down the favored home team. The fans and announcers spewed hatred our way, yet the worse they got, the more fired up we became.

The game was tight all night. Every single play could have counted for the win. It was back and forth, grimy, a slugfest. Big defensive stands contrasted with huge offensive plays, peppered with even bigger questionable calls. The game was a battle, but in the end, Springer would not be denied, and with her score, we won in overtime. Unimaginable! Many argue it was one of the best games in the history of women's football.

I watched the film later. When you're in a game, you're emotionally wrapped up. To step outside and go back and listen allowed me to relive those moments, relive the fight, on the edge of my seat even though I knew the outcome. The announcers stood out because they were supposed to be impartial, but clearly they were not. They started the game mispronouncing all of the Diamonds' names. It sunk in as I listened just how one-sided the expectations had been for that game. The broadcasters knew everything about Chicago and nothing about us.

Somewhere in the middle they started picking up on us— you could hear it in their voices. The shift. By the end, they were screaming with enthusiasm. *Number forty-seven Jen Welter is on fire!* They called me "the defensive workhorse of the Dallas Diamonds." That game changed the course of my life.

COACH JEN:
KEEP PUSHING AND FIND YOUR THING

Sometimes finding and holding onto that place in the world where you know you're the best, where you know you're great, where you can find your sanity and quiet among chaos can pull you through so you can start to be that champion in other areas of your life as well. If I didn't have football, I might have lost that belief in myself during that hard time. Eventually, my ability translated into other areas of my life when I cleared some of the chaos. I drew on my behavior on the field elsewhere. Here's how you can do the same:

- Find the place where you're whole and invincible and make it your own. It's not about anybody else in your life. It's only about you and your dream, and only you know when to hold tight and keep at it. Football was for me and for the insiders playing with me—not for the outside world's approval. We had sanctity in our inner circle.

- Confidence is contagious. If you find greatness in one place, it will spread. It will slowly infuse your life and let you believe that you can do anything in other areas.

- Work hard and you'll see results. You'll start to feel good about yourself in one area and you'll take things on in other areas.

- Do big things or small things, but do something that is yours and only yours.

- Remember that your team is bigger than you. On the days I might have given up for myself, I showed up for my team. I played for something bigger.

That sanctuary that I had in football made me play that Chicago championship like my life depended on it because it did. But the people who loved me thought I was crazy to continue to chase my football dream any further. Though the details of my relationship with my then-fiancé weren't exactly fully out in the open, those who knew me knew things had ended badly. They wanted me to have a safe and normal life. My friends suggested I give up football. Their words came from a good place. What they didn't realize was that football pulled me through the toughest parts of my life. The harder things got off the field, the more I needed football. The only time things felt *together* was on the football field. Chaos swallowed up everything else, but on the field, I could do anything. On the field, I knew exactly what I was supposed to do. On the field, I was larger than life, even though I was so small people often called me "kid."

That game topped off the season in which I went from playing football to being a football player. I had fought harder for that win and that season, just to stay in the game, than for anything I'd ever fought for before. Years after getting my first $12 check, and despite the wins, my financial picture was still rocky, and my life still hadn't sorted itself out in the traditional sense, but my football career was holding me together.

COACH JEN: NEVER QUIT

The people who urge you to quit your dream are the ones who don't understand the importance it holds for you. They don't know the full value of your dreams. Football was that one place in my life where I was good. The rest of my life was chaos. But I could step onto that field and I could leave all that badness and all that worry behind. No drama, no stress, no matter how bad it got, went with me onto that field. I would leave the rest of the world behind, step on the field, and step into greatness.

Digging Out

In addition to clinging to football, and maybe because of it, I dug out of the mess in my life one small step at a time. When you're in a rut or struggling, simply put, you have to be willing to keep going no matter what happens or what obstacles appear in front of you. That's the key to digging out no matter how dire it all feels or how deep you're in it. There's not always some big, grand master plan. You won't always see the solution. I certainly didn't. I knew only that I had to keep going.

On some days, when I didn't think I could do much more, I did just one little thing to repair my life. Some days, I tackled everything possible. Either way, I didn't get hung up on what was or wasn't possible long term; rather, I took a tiny step each day. Small steps or big steps, no matter what, I showed up. I went to work. I went to practice. I put one foot in front of the other as I rebuilt. Eventually, those baby steps decreased in number, and the number of days I tackled grew. Eventually, it all added up.

Think about a long-term goal or a situation you need to change that requires multiple steps over a course of months. You can dig out and fix part of the problem in just one day or even one week. If every day you do one thing toward that goal—one phone call, one hour of research, one box packed, one file cleared out—eventually all of those tiny steps add up. A call may provide a lead. Just getting out of bed and going for a walk might boost your spirits and inspire you to do that research. Step by step. One foot in front of the other. Eventually, change happens. Lots of tiny changes equal big life changes.

COACH JEN: MAKE SURE YOU SHOW UP

- Find people who will support you. Not everyone will. Know the difference. Believe me, I leaned on the wrong people along the way, but learning how that played out made me more careful in the future.

- Enlist the help of friends any time you can and call your family.

- Realize and really believe in your bones that you are not defined by who you were but by who you are going to be.

- Sitting still is absolutely not an option.

- Don't stay down after getting tackled. Get up and make plays.

The bottom line is to be aware that any progress you make in a day is good progress. If you hit a wall heading in one direction, change course and make progress one inch over in another direction. Just be certain you continue to try. Some days you'll see huge improvements. Some days just tiny improvements. Ultimately, it will all add up to change.

In the bad times you'll learn a lot about yourself, too. I did. As I dug out, I was able to more objectively reflect on my life off the field and understand the importance of what I was doing on the field. In struggle, there is insight. I realized that my relationship with my fiancé wasn't about my own failure. I thought it was my responsibility to help him and fix him and fix us—to make things work. Thinking of marrying him made me sick, but we had a house and dogs. We felt committed. But what I learned, finally, was that there's a very big difference between a bad situation and a dream. In the midst of my passion for football and for school, I took my eye off the relationship ball and was seeing what I wanted to see versus what was actually in front of me. Learning to see a situation clearly became a pivotal lesson for me, and though it was painful, it was powerful.

Confirmation to Hang In

Quitting was never an option for me, and my fortitude proved to have positive effects.

The long-term implications of that championship game in Chicago eventually revealed themselves. John Konecki, the head coach of the Chicago Force for the 2008 championship game, went on to coach the first-ever Women's National Tackle Football Team. I had made an impression on Konecki. He hated playing against me, so when he had a chance to have me on his team, he did.

In 2010, the United States fielded Team USA in the inaugural IFAF Women's World Championship. Never before had there been a women's Team USA for football. There wasn't a glimmer of hope for it because it didn't exist. We didn't know to pray or strive for such a dream because it had never been dreamed before. Then, suddenly, a national women's team created to represent the United States of America abroad. That was a major, unexpected, and unforeseen breakthrough! I wanted to be a part of it.

I will never forget the day I got the call that I made the USA National Team. It was one of the greatest days of my life and I was honored and humbled to have been chosen to play among this exceptional roster of women, the best team in the world.

It was a high compliment and, at the same time, a harsh reality.

Congratulations, you are one of the best female players in the world. You will represent your country. Now, to do that, you have to cut us a check for about $3,000 and take a month off work.

To bring home the gold, we each had to sacrifice income and come up with almost $3,000 because there was no funding to send us to compete for our country. We had to pay to play, as always.

Even when you have a breakthrough, sometimes it's not easy. Sadly, that was the reality of wearing red, white, and blue for our country. Though it was a huge honor, some of the players simply could not afford it. Others could, but most of us used a combination of fund-raising, sponsorships, family, friends, and essentially any means necessary to make it happen.

Faced with that kind of challenge, some people might have said, "No, not me." But we'd spent so many years conditioned to be where we weren't supposed to be, doing something we were never supposed to do, that we were honored to be a part of creating change and writing history. We were remaking the rulebook and doing something that defied odds and that had never been done.

When you're already defying the odds, you do whatever it takes—go further, push harder, accept less to receive a greater payoff. You embrace the breakthroughs as they arrive and the challenges that come with them because there will often be the breakdown just before you break out into greatness.

PLAYING FOR Team USA was a new experience. It was the first time in my life I could actually focus 100 percent on football. When we reported to training camp in Round Rock, Texas, we left everything else outside the game. We were, for the first time, full-time football players. The 2010 Women's National Tackle Football Team had a singular focus: becoming the best football team in the world and bringing home a gold medal. No outside juggling of jobs and kids and boyfriends and life was permitted to distract us.

We entered training camp with gold medal dreams, but we had work to do to become a team. We had our own alliances from our pasts, and each of us made those team alliances known when we rolled into camp. Individual team colors and logos marked hard lines of separation. Rivalries were in full effect.

To say that it was awkward to have to play with members of the team we had just defeated is the ultimate understatement. Three days prior, my job had been to sack Chicago quarterback Sami Grisafe. But that day in Round Rock, she and I were teammates. There was no way to tell how this would play out, but to their credit, the Team USA coaches set the tone quickly: first, no individual team gear was tolerated. We were playing for Team USA, and the Red, White, and Blue were the only colors that mattered. We were expected to get to know each other, and we were not permitted to room with anyone from our own team. Rooms would be assigned. No requests. No discussion.

One Team: One Mission. That was our motto, and we all bought in completely. This was history. Never before had there been an International Federation of American Football Women's World Championship. Six nations would compete: Austria, Finland, Sweden, Germany, Canada, and the USA.

As the first Team USA, we had to prepare to be the very best team in the world, with little knowledge of whom we were preparing for. There was no game film of our opponents because they had never played together before either.

Those hundred-plus-degree days in Round Rock broke us down and brought us together. When we boarded the flights to Stockholm, Sweden, there was no more division, there were no remnants of our individual team colors, we were all business, each one of us with Red, White, and Blue in our veins. And we came home with a gold medal in America's game. We had set the standard for what the game would look like for women.

IN 2013 WHEN the opportunity to represent Team USA arose, of course, I wanted back in. I went to the tryouts and made the team. That was around the same time that I graduated with my PhD in psychology. Yet again I had to come up with $3,000 and take a month off work, but this time, I was pissed off about it. I decided I would raise my $3,000 by raising awareness about the truth of playing for Team USA.

For the first time, I was getting past my individual ego. I was admitting weakness. Early in my career, I refused to admit that our "professional football player" title came with only a $1 per game paycheck. I just couldn't take it anymore. I realized that my refusal to ask for help had ultimately not helped me, and it also had not helped the game I loved. I started to tell the story of women's football on a bigger scale. I started a blog and pitched it for publicity, and the response was amazing: people actually stepped up to help. By asking for help, I raised the entire amount required for me to play for Team USA.

When I reported to training camp, I felt like I had a team of people cheering for me, because they had a vested interest. The blog became so popular that *USA Football* asked me to write to cover the Women's World Championship. So much for being 100 percent focused on football! Somehow, yet again, I had managed to create another job for myself. However, I was willing to do it, because I wanted to change the game. I really believed if people knew about the women of Team USA, they would fall in love with us.

Our 2013 team committed to making a statement to the world: women in the USA will play football, and we will not be denied.

Despite hardships, despite having to fund-raise, and despite having to wear those white practice jerseys while representing our country, we left no doubt that American football is America's game. American WOMEN are the best football players in the world. The need to declare our independence and our dominance resonated with the entire team.

We again won a gold medal in America's game. And yet, again, it seemed no one even knew we existed. Not one major media outlet covered our story. The White House Council of Women and Girls was the only institution that recognized our progress. Imagining that we had finally cracked a significant barrier for women in football, I wrote a story about the team and our reception at the White House. Unfortunately, we couldn't even get that story published.

The underlying message was clear: women's football was not newsworthy. As far as we had come, we still had a long way to go. And two gold medals were not enough to do it. It would take something drastic. I clung to my drive and fortitude and carried on.

We all have defining moments in life. To step into your destiny, you have to be willing to stand up for yourself and for what you believe in. Determine what defines you and the legacy you'll leave.

||||||||||||||||||||||||||||||||||||||||||||||||||||||||||||||||||||||||||||||||||

7

Once It's Been Done, It Can't Be Undone

It is completely normal to fear failure. Every person who has dared to step outside his or her comfort zone and the safety of what's always been done has had that little voice of doubt, that little devil on the shoulder, whisper, "What if you fail? What will they say if you can't do it?" Trust me, at each defining moment in my life, I heard that voice. Loud. Clear. However, the best way I found to silence that voice in my head was to literally smile and get it done. You see, when I started to question whether or not I could do something or what would happen if I failed, I realized that if I tried my best and I did not succeed, I could live with that. What I could not live with was always wondering what would have happened if . . .? Take your shot and make the most of it. Many of the defining moments in your life will be tests—tests of your strength, your bravery, your character. Take those tests and make the most of them. Realize that people will use you if you let them, but you have the opportunity to use every opportunity when you take it and run. Hanging in there paid off for me. In fact, it started a revolution.

FOR MUCH OF my football career, people asked if my goal was to play in the NFL. I would immediately laugh and say, "I'm five-foot-two and 130 pounds. I would never do that. I'm not crazy."

Apparently, God has a sense of humor. Or maybe he, like me, doesn't like the word *never* because, as it turns out, I wasn't going to play in the NFL, but I was going to play against men. My destiny was mapped out. And I was crazy enough to step up.

Around the same time I was coming off of my second Team USA gold medal, enthusiastic and proud that I'd hung in there with my football dream, I received bad news: the Diamonds were folding. Our football dynasty was officially coming to an abrupt end, leaving its players with no team and feeling lost as we tried to figure out what to do next.

In the midst of this transformative time, I got a phone call from Tommy Benezio, the president of the Texas Revolution. The Revolution played in the Indoor Football League, a men's professional league that plays in small arenas across the country. He reached out and asked me for a meeting. I was not exactly sure what Tommy wanted when he called, but I agreed to see him.

When I showed up at the Revolution offices, the difference between men's pro football funding and women's was immediately apparent. It wasn't the NFL, but it was certainly a step up. The floor was actually painted to look like a football field, and the back wall was painted to look as if there were fans in the stands all wearing Texas Revolution T-shirts. The place felt flashy, pretty, and like the walls were full of team spirit in stark opposition to the world of the Diamonds. The Diamonds' office—well, we had no office. We operated out of the owner's house.

Tommy greeted me, as did the head coach of the Revolution, Chris Williams. I won't lie—Tommy was welcoming, but Coach seemed to be a reluctant participant. We assembled at a table with the painted fans watching, almost as if they were behind Tommy cheering us on.

Coach made it clear through his body language that he wanted to be anywhere but there as he drew in his nonexistent playbook. His right arm was wrapped around his notepad, making it so he almost had his back to me. His level of disinterest was offset by Tommy's nervous and excited energy.

"Jen," Tommy said, kicking things off, "I think it would be really cool to have you come to training camp for a day and go through the drills with some of our guys. Get some media, you know."

My brain started firing not great thoughts: *Go through some drills with the guys? A day of training camp? Was he serious? What would be the point of that and why would I want to be paraded out there like that? I am absolutely not going to be some sort of PR stunt.*

"As in, run some ladder drills for cameras?" I asked.

He nodded.

As is often the case in my life, words came firing out of my mouth long before my brain had my thoughts in order.

"Absolutely not," I said. "That doesn't respect the game of football or me as an athlete, not to mention that your guys would absolutely hate it. If you want me to do anything with your football team, either I do all of training camp, step for step, hit for hit, or I do nothing at all."

This was a defining moment. I felt my life shift with those words, and I had just stepped into my destiny. As the words came out of my mouth I had spoken it into existence. The reality sent a ripple through my spirit and left the hair on the back of my neck tingling with energy like static electricity. I knew it was going to happen. I knew I'd drawn a line and I knew which side I'd land on. I had my mouth and my words to thank for that, but I just knew it. I was going to play football against men.

I also knew I might get killed doing it.

Within seconds things got real. I had just said unequivocally that I wanted to crack the glass ceiling on a sport owned by men—shattering the notion of a simple photo-op with pro men football players. I had thrown down the gauntlet, making clear this was an all-or-nothing situation and that I was going onto that field to take hit after hit with the men or I wasn't going onto that field. What was I thinking?

There was a pause, or maybe it just felt like there was, because the world was moving in slow motion.

My words created two opposing reactions. Coach, who had been physically present but mentally elsewhere, was suddenly engaged, as if a switch had been flipped. Tommy looked shell-shocked and distant, like my words had hit him in the face like a hard high five.

Coach tipped his chin to me and cracked a half smile. While I'd horrified the team owner, I'd made an opening with the coach. There was anxiety and fear in that room, but there was also my love of the game.

COACH JEN:
THE SECRET MAGIC OF LOVE AND FEAR

When something gets you pumped up, you know you're alive. Physiologically, the symptoms of anxiety and excitement are exactly the same. Your palms get sweaty. Your heart races. It's your body's way of letting you know it's go-time. The only difference between the two is how you interpret the signs in your mind. That's important. We don't fear things we don't care about. There's a fine line between the two. It's like love and hate—you have to have loved something to have the passion to hate it, or else you're experiencing apathy. Emotions, such as fear, excitement, and love, signal that something is important. I loved the game of football. I feared what would happen if they put me on the field with men. Still, there was no other choice. And sometimes your first instinct—the way you react before you have a chance to think further or take it back—is the right one.

Though he was in shock, Tommy proceeded. "Um, Coach, do you think she would be too much of a distraction for the guys if she competed through the entire training camp?"

Coach Williams looked Tommy straight in the face and said, "Hell no, with an attitude like that, she might be the best thing in the world for these guys. She'd give them a kick in the ass. And, assuming she survives, she might just bring the team together."

I smiled and, in the same moment, Coach turned to me and listed off expectations. "You go through just like the guys. I will treat you just like the guys. You get no special treatment from me. Every hit. Step for step. If you sidestep one drill, I'm gonna cut you. And I am going to tell the guys the same damn thing. You are all fighting for jobs. If a guy sidesteps you, so help me, I will cut him on the spot." As he kept going, I replied "Yes, Coach" to each point he made.

"Frankly," he said, "I don't think you're going to make it."

"I don't know either, Coach."

"I have seen your film, and you are tough, but you are far too light in the ass to play linebacker with these boys. You will get run straight over. You are going to have to play running back with us. Can you do that?"

"Honestly, I am more scared to play running back than I am to play with men."

"Well, that's the only way it's going to work."

"You're the coach."

Later in his office we continued our conversation. Coach Williams shook his head. "Never in my life did I think I would see this. Girl, you are going to get hit. Hell, you might just get killed out there. But if you survive, we just might be doing something really special with this football team. Just imagine, what if you were able to stick it out all year with the team . . . even practice squad for a whole season?"

We both nodded, and I looked up directly into his eyes, making a silent promise to God, myself, him, and every girl who ever loved football. "If they want me off this team, they will have to kick me off or kill me, because I sure as hell am not quitting."

I absorbed the gravity and historic significance of the moment. Looking back at that meeting, I took more from the situation than they had intended to give me. It would have been very easy to agree to go through a day of training camp with the guys, then promptly return to the women's league. This was a pivot—a turning point. And I hadn't even really meant to or set out to do it.

To break through a glass ceiling, sometimes you have to apply force to the smallest crack and see what happens. After all, it just might shatter.

COACH JEN: SHATTER IT

- If an opportunity presents itself, grab it and shatter a ceiling.

- It doesn't matter how you get your foot in the door, kick ass when you do!

- Just because you didn't go looking for an opportunity doesn't mean you shouldn't grab it when one reveals itself.

- When you have a chance to turn a meeting into an unexpected opportunity—and women don't do this as much as men do—snatch it. Men often jump into a situation and learn what they need to know when they get there. Women overprepare and often pass up opportunities because they feel like they're not ready. Sometimes you just have to be bold enough to say, "You know what? I'm going to take it as it comes," and to push yourself into those opportunities that push the envelope.

- Pursue your passion, but realize that it's not always going to be pretty. It's not going to fit in the box. It's not going to go by anybody else's standards. Your choices are either to quit or to keep moving forward, and if you keep moving forward—by inches or in leaps and bounds—you're successful. You can't predict what success looks like, and you can't get mad at yourself for not foreseeing certain things in this world.

What If I Fumble?

As I drove away from that meeting I knew it could take months to find out if I made the team and would sign with them. Though I was excited about my future with the Revolution, in the meantime, I had a life to get on with.

Also, lingering fear following me out of the meeting: I believed in what was happening, but doubt crept in. I had no guarantee that it was going to work out or that I'd make the cut if it did. I had to formulate a backup plan, and I settled on the Houston Energy women's team as my second option.

Several months went by with no communication. Just as I was thinking about the Energy, I got an email from the Revolution.

They wanted to schedule another meeting to work out the details of signing me to training camp so they could mention it at their upcoming press conference.

The rush of emotions was so complex it's hard even now to identify what I was feeling. A mix of shock, excitement, amazement, and terror. Never mind the insecurity and fear I had about being on the field, my life was about to change and my football life was going to head in an unexpected direction.

I explored my expectations around playing football with the men. My mind went to two of my favorite people, two of the best women's players in the world, my teammates of forever, Berta and Odessa. Berta and Odessa both played running back, and both were more skilled at it than I was. Either one of them would have been better matched to step into the Revolution's training camp.

For a time, my mind said I should hand the opportunity off to Odessa or Berta and let one of them run with it. I did not want to be selfish or greedy. I finally let them in on what was happening and told them they were much better suited to play running back against men than I, but neither one would take the opportunity.

"You can't hand off your destiny," Odessa said. "You were chosen for a reason. This is your shot, take the ball and run with it. This is what we've been fighting for."

"Welty," Berta said, "why won't you do it? I believe in you, and you already know I've got your back."

Their words had an impact. In my career, when playing women's football, I took the field with and against the absolute best women in the game. They were stellar and inspiring, all of them working hard at a sport they loved. So, when the opportunity to play with men in a position other than as a kicker—where women had already kicked down barriers and scored major points—presented itself, I thought it was a little odd that I'd been the one called on because there were many players who were better suited. At the time, I had enough confidence to know I was one of the best in the game, but I didn't ever believe I was *the* best, and I surely was not as a running back. I came to understand why I should not give in to the urge to hand off the opportunity to other players. Those same players were the first to tell me to take the shot and run with it. In fact, later they were the ones cheering loudest for me at the game when I did.

When opportunity presents itself, you have to accept it for what it is and take it. You might not recognize it at first as an opportunity, or a realistic one, because sometimes the best chances show up in disguise. What looks like a challenge might be an opportunity. What looks terrifying might be an opportunity. What looks like a wrong turn might just be the right one. Accept that thing that crosses your path even if it doesn't always feel completely on the mark. Have confidence enough to know there's a reason you're being called on for a task, a project, or a job. Don't let fear or questioning of your skills stop you. Trust it. Take it on. Be confident, and know you were chosen for a reason.

Having said that, I won't lie: I was afraid. I was afraid to fumble, in a literal and metaphorical sense. I am a woman, and a small one at that. So there was a chance I would get in the game, take my shot at history, and not only get tackled but also lose the ball completely. The worst football outcome possible, other than not being able to get up again, was to lose the ball and have the other team recover it. Still, I knew that the greater fumble would've been refusing to take the ball in the first place.

In football, I had played defense and preferred it. I was the long shot to do what I was being asked to do, to put myself in the position of getting tackled by men. Yes, even I knew this was crazy. I feel fear, too, remember! However, I would rather try my best than live life wondering what might have happened. Had I passed on the opportunity, I would have thought about the what-ifs every single day. I refused then and I refuse now to let fear of the unknown stop me.

TRAILBLAZING WOMEN IN MEN'S FOOTBALL

Patricia Palinkas was a holder back in the very early seventies. Julie Harshbarger and Katharine Hnida were kickers in 2010. Lisa Horton played quarterback for the men's semipro club, the Pittsburgh Colts, and she threw a touchdown pass in one game. In 1996, my former teammate with the Mass Mutiny Carley Pesente tried out for the Minnesota Fighting Pike, which was a pro team in the Arena Football League. Recently, Becca Longo kicked down another huge barrier when she became the first female to earn a college football scholarship by signing with Adams State. With record numbers of girls playing high school football, it will be exciting to see the trailblazing continue.

I am sure there are trailblazers whose names I could not find, just as I am sure there will be names we will hear in the future. To all of you, I take my helmet off in respect.

Seeing the Bigger Picture with Humor

As soon as I committed to play for the Texas Revolution, I knew I was living my destiny.

Playing with men was not what I set out to do. It was actually something I had said I would never do, and I was not even sure I was capable of doing it. There was nothing about this choice that made sense to anyone else, and if I would have sat down and weighed the pros and cons from a strictly intellectual and practical standpoint, it would not have made sense to me either. However, to the core of my spirit, I knew it was right. This was the same feeling I had when I made my first football team. This was my next great challenge to follow the game as far as it would take me.

If you believe in destiny, that means you believe in something bigger than yourself. Even if using the word *destiny* isn't your thing, maybe you believe in a higher purpose or a higher calling, or just the idea that you have particular gifts to offer in this life. With that you have to have faith and be willing to listen to that inner voice of courage and strength, to seize a fleeting moment or opportunity, and to know that you are capable of that higher calling.

What are the things in your life that define you, that make you hungry and bold, make you feel ten feet tall? What things make your world a greater place and make you greater within your place in the world? Picture the love and strength of a mother who lifts a car off her child to save his life. Now channel that love, passion, strength, and faith into the capabilities that you have in your life that you have yet to tap into. You are capable of moving a mountain in the direction of your destiny. You may not even have thought it possible, and to feel it, you have to be willing to shed the pretense, strip off the layers of perceived limitation and expectation, and truly listen to that voice, the one that sometimes whispers, and trust the goosebumps that manifest with the possibility. Let that whisper and those goosebumps give you the courage to step into greatness.

In joining the Revolution, I was hearing the whispers and the yells, too. I saw the bigger picture of my destiny and what an important step it was for girls and women. I was excited about shattering the glass ceiling. The decision was already made. The momentum had been building. I was going to sign, and I was going to play.

A press conference to announce me joining the team was scheduled. Already I was hearing the rumblings of opinions, both praise and criticism, online, yet they were distant and often anonymous and did not faze me. The Internet is an intense breeding ground for scrutiny. It is amazing the things people will say with the security of anonymity. One person commented: She's going to get hit and die and get pregnant. When I read that, I laughed out loud. What else could I do?

This statement became my answer to disarming any naysayers. Rather than waiting for reporters to ask about it, I told them it was the worst criticism I ever got. Then I explained that I was one of the best linebackers in the game and that I hit people really hard, but that even I didn't know it was possible to hit someone so hard that you could cause immaculate conception and death! Interviewers came to love that deflection and laughed about as hard as I did. Humor could disarm and charm them all. I ended up using it on some of my greatest critics.

COACH JEN: BE CONFIDENT

We have power—both positive and negative—over ourselves in unimaginable ways. It's easy to get inside our own heads and defeat ourselves in all sorts of situations. Had I not overcome my insecurity and fear and tapped deep into my confidence I would not be where I am today. Here are some ways to boost your confidence:

- Own your impact: you are the most powerful influencer you know.

- Exhibit confidence even when you're sweating a situation.

- React positively to challenges.

- Play sports—join a league or play a sport you used to enjoy as a kid. You'll learn a lot about yourself and team building and boost your confidence along the way.

- Take setbacks in stride. Learn from them and step over them.

- Take a moment to congratulate yourself even for small wins you experience in a day.

  And: Inspire Confidence in Others

  People can be fragile. Often they need a boost to help them find their own confidence. As a leader, you can inspire that confidence in others with a few simple strategies:

- Lead by example. Set an example for young people. Show them you're confident in your decision making by sticking to a plan, not being intimidated.

- Compliment others on their determination and persistence, not just their physical appearance.

- Put your kids—especially young girls—in sports, too. Girls start to lose confidence around puberty, but sports can boost it.

- Remember that we're all in this together. We're stronger as a whole.

Calling in Support

Sometimes, even all the confidence we can muster isn't enough, and we need to call on our trusted supporters to reassure us of our destiny.

The night before that big press conference announcing I was playing for the Revolution, I needed to talk to my mom and dad. I needed my hero, my dad, a Vietnam veteran with a Silver Star and two Bronze Stars, to reassure me.

Over the years, I learned the meaning of bravery through his stories of the war. With each tale, I would envision my very own GI Joe, or GI Daddy, as he described pulling people from burning tanks, the bounty on his head, the Asian Pit Vipers, and the enemies deep in the heart of the jungle. My dad was larger than life to me, and those early stories shaped my mentality.

"I was the best warrior," he'd say, "because I didn't allow negativity to come into the matrix." He explained how when he first showed up at the "dance," which is what they called the war, he was intimidated because, as a combat medic, he had received no real infantry training. "The longer I was there, the better I got, and ultimately there was no one better in the woods than me."

Knowing that my dad had faced what seemed like insurmountable lack of preparation and also fatal danger, I learned as a child to be fearless. His fearlessness stayed with me ever since.

That night before the press conference, I called my parents, and they put me on speaker phone.

"Guys, I have some other news I want to share," I said. "I would hate for you to be caught off guard or hear it elsewhere first. There is a press conference this Friday to announce that I will be the first woman to play running back in men's professional football." I was all business, as my dad had taught me: never show fear.

"Do they have insurance in case you get hurt?" my mother asked. Before I could even answer "Yes, Mom," my dad said, "Jenny won't get hurt. She's a tough cookie like her popsie."

Tears of pride and joy and thankfulness and pure love welled up in my eyes. The fear left my body. Surely, if something bad was going to happen, he never would let me do it.

I had my reassurance. My dad would not have let me enter unknown territory if I was going to be a casualty in the trenches. I believed he would sense imminent danger and warn me, just like he had done for his fellow soldiers in Vietnam. So, with no warning, I had no fear. What I did have was faith. Faith that I was doing what I was meant to do.

Stepping Up My Game

It had been a long time since I tried out for a football team. Other than Team USA, where we were all trying out and trying each other, I had been with the Dallas Diamonds for ten years. I wasn't a rookie; I was a vet. I was the one who was testing the new girls. Now that I was about to be the one tested, I couldn't help but think back to that first Diamonds tryout.

The Diamonds were a team on the rise. They were a tight group, and they did not take kindly to outsiders or rookies. Worse, I was a rival. I had led the other Dallas team, the Dragons, in tackles. They clearly sent a message in the tryout to see what I was made of. They all wanted a piece of the new girl, and I knew it. In fact, I welcomed it. I knew I was good, and I wanted a piece of them, too.

In each drill back then, I was mysteriously pulling the veterans, and they were going hard. As practice went on, the hits kept coming, and the tone was changing. I was not backing down. I was bringing it. Then we went to more live action, and it happened. I tackled the running back, Jessica Springer. All of a sudden I heard, *Oh shit, new girl took down Springer.* At the time, I didn't know who Springer was, but I quickly came to realize Springer was THE running back. In all my years playing, Springer was by far one of the greatest female players to ever play the game, and she was the cornerstone of the Dallas Diamonds dynasty as we went on to win four championships. But on that day, that tackle solidified my place as a member of their team and a part of the dynasty we'd build together. At the end of practice, they took my silver helmet and painted it black. From Mass Mutiny gold, to Dallas Dragons silver, to championship color, Dallas Diamonds black.

Just as I had at that tryout, now I was stepping up my game and stepping into the men's game. I was entering Texas Revolution territory. Though the sex of my opponents was different and the level of play was higher, I knew the tests would be the same. I needed to take the hits and earn my place on the team.

As I prepared to take the field with the men, I strapped up my black helmet with the purple Diamonds logo on the side. I was bringing my sisters with me. This was for them. At the end of training camp, if I had earned their respect, earned my place on the team, and earned my place in history, I would retire that black helmet and adopt the Revolution's white one with stars down the middle and a cannon on the side. That would be fitting because, after all, we were starting a Revolution.

I played thirteen years of women's football and became one of the best in the world, with two gold medals, and nobody even knew I existed until I took big hits from men.

|||||||||||||||||||||||||||||||||||||||||||||||||||||||||||||||||||||||||||||||||

8

Winning in the Boys' Club

What most people don't realize is that a perfect tackle doesn't hurt, to give it or to receive it. Yes, there is contact, yes, there is impact, but a good clean tackle is exhilarating. Good clean tacklers are masters of the takedown, and most of the time, those getting tackled, get right back up. There is a code followed by most football players that we want to win, but not permanently injure our opponents. Injuries are more often a result of bad luck and bad form than bad intentions. Players with bad intentions usually don't last too long, because by making others targets, they make themselves targets. Without that basic respect and trust, on any play almost any player could be taken out. There is a big difference between making the play and targeting the player.

FOOTBALL PLAYERS TEST each other to see what they're made of. Going less than 100 percent against someone is not a compliment. It's actually an insult. It's like saying, "you can't handle my best." I always wanted to get someone's best because I can promise you they were going to get mine.

My first practice with the Texas Revolution guys was grueling.

One drill in particular—picking up the blitzing linebacker—put me on my butt, over and over and over and over. Just when I thought I got it, the linebacker would give me a swim move, and I would swim through the air, then swim through the dirt, as if I were sliding into home base.

Though I landed on everything but my feet, something unexpected was occurring: the guys were amazing and open to what was happening. I hadn't gone in feeling overly defensive, but I still wasn't sure how well I would be received on the field. Drill after drill, as competitive as everyone was, I was amazed to see they were equally supportive of me. It was an exhilarating and eye-opening experience. It was an unexpected lesson for everyone entering an unknown situation. I gave it my best and made it clear I was one of them. No special treatment. No worries about dirt or landing in it. Nothing different. Period.

I was establishing my boundaries, too. In every situation you face when you're the odd woman out, you'll be tested. I was being tested physically, but also in other ways. They were checking my attitude, too. The guys needed to know they could be themselves around me. They needed to know I could literally roll with the punches in more ways than one. I was taking hits on the football field, but I needed to be able to roll with the mental jabs as well. They wanted to see how I bounced back.

During one practice, the running back coach asked a simple question: "Hey, running backs, do you all have your balls?" One of the linebackers answered, "Yeah, all but Jen."

It was a defining moment. There was silence in anticipation of my response. I jogged over to the guy who had said it, smiled, patted him on the shoulder pads, and said, "That's okay, baby. When I need balls I'll just grab yours from your wife's purse."

Everyone lost it. Victory for me and relief for them. They knew I could hold my own, on the field and off. In a way, I was one of the guys, even though they respected that I was a woman. In an interview one of my six-foot-eight teammates who was nicknamed Big Country said in a deep Southern accent, "Just because she doesn't have our parts doesn't mean she isn't part of the team."

The Locker Room Handles Itself

There is a difference between going hard against someone—with jokes, jabs, or physical force in a scrimmage—and undermining a teammate. Certain behavior is not acceptable and needs to be handled for a team to have harmony. Joining the Revolution was when I learned what the phrase *the locker room handles itself* really meant.

Sometimes it takes only one person or player to change the entire dynamic, and in this case it was our number one receiver, who wore number 1. He came to me before training camp began and introduced himself. "My name is Clinton Solomon, or you can just call me Solo. First let me say, I am happy to have you here. I checked you out, and you are a legit ball player. I think you are incredibly brave, and I've got your back. I have been playing football a long time, and I want you to know, you are the best thing that has happened to the IFL since I have been here."

I smiled and said, "The best thing? I doubt that."

"I'm serious," he said. "Today is like this because of you. You see these numbers? They are about double the normal amount. That's 'cause of you. You see these fans? I've never seen fans at a tryout. You see these sponsors? I've never seen them before either. And you see these cameras? Baby girl, they're here for you. And frankly, I think I am the smartest guy here."

I laughed and asked him why.

"Superstar, I am right next to you, and I'm gonna stay in your hip pocket so I'm in all the pictures." He flashed his million-dollar smile, put his arm around me, and I smiled back up at him.

"No matter what, I've got you. This will not be easy, but you are not alone. And remember this, the locker room handles itself. If anyone gives you a hard time, I will handle it. Don't you dare let any guy see he has gotten to you. You be invincible and unaffected, and it sends a message, and at the same time, I will send a message about what will not be tolerated."

I took his advice to heart. He knew that it was going to get rough out there. Solo asked for the chance to be the veteran leader in the locker room, to be the one to draw the line in the sand, to step up and set the tone, and I was going to let him. Why turn down an ally? If the locker room could handle itself, then I would let it.

A few days into training camp, Solo jogged up to me. "Little mama, don't you worry about him, I've got this." I had no idea what he was talking about. I hadn't heard, but apparently a cornerback did not want me out there, and he was loudly proclaiming that he was going to take me out if I ran his way. Solo got everyone's attention. "Coach, I need some one-on-ones." Then he pointed at the mouthy corner. "You are not good enough to talk shit to a girl. I'm going to get you cut today."

Solo lined up, and the corner walked up to attempt press coverage. Solo looked to the QB and gave the signal for a fade route, then looked at the corner and smiled. "I'm taking this one to the house."

At least ten times in a row Solo lined up for one-on-ones against the corner. Each time he would look at the quarterback, call the route he was about to run; then proceed to catch the pass, present the ball to him, and send a clear message to him and to every player on that team. Solo was the number one receiver on the team, and the number one person had my back. The rest of the team followed his lead. The corner was cut from the team for failing to cover him on all those plays. As Solo had promised, the locker room handled itself.

The truth was that the guys also needed to see me get knocked down so that they could extend a hand of respect and help me up. The great thing about those guys was they not only helped me back up but also helped me get better. To live your dream you have to be willing to get knocked down, and when you get back up and keep fighting hard, you earn respect.

When I played with the guys, I was not a great running back. But I was brave enough to take the hits every day. I never complained, and I worked my ass off. That's what the guys needed to see to converge around me in support—that and to know that a leader among them, my friend Solo, trusted me enough to have my back. They didn't need me to run past them every play. They didn't need me to run through them. They needed to see that I was never going to quit, that I wasn't going to complain, that when they took their best shots, I would roll with the punches, physically and mentally. Eventually they realized I belonged, and then we all got along and quickly became a team and then a family.

COACH JEN:
RULES TO MAKING IT IN THE BOYS' CLUB

- Get in the door any which way you can. Doesn't matter how as long as you kick butt once you do.

- Find someone on the inside to bet on you.

- Show your street cred—let your game film, whatever that is in your world, speak for you.

- Be authentic.

- Don't tell them to listen to you; make them want to.

- Get in the mix and show what you know. Find your style and contribute. Don't be nervous to dive in.

- You can be treated like one of the guys while still commanding respect as a woman. In other words, you can work hard and prove yourself even in situations when all eyes are on you for being different.

On the football field, and in life, we all get knocked down, so really, what matters is how you respond. I had heard the whispers, as well as the rants, and I knew everyone on the Revs and in the media wanted to see how I would respond to getting hit by the men. Would I die after getting hit the first time? Guess what? I lived. Would I be broken after the first day of pads? Guess what? I never felt more alive. Why? Because I was living my dream and earning respect along the way. People needed to see me get whooped a few times to realize that I was not going to slow down, break down, quit, cry, or go less than 100 percent.

Oh, and for the record, they also needed to see that I could light a few people up and that I was a little "pitbull" on the football field. Though I knew that going in, it didn't make transitioning from the great atmosphere of the training camp into game time any easier.

Get Back Up No Matter What

It was Game Day: My men's professional football debut.

I pushed open the locker room door and was greeted by a wave of glitter. It was surreal. This was unlike any locker room I had ever been in. My eyes adjusted, and I realized it was not an illusion or delirium. It was reality. The Revolution dancers were literally glittering each other. It was as if Sephora had exploded; there were pom-pom fragments and beauty products everywhere. This was the antithesis of any locker room I had ever been in.

As I struggled to get my bearings, one dancer grabbed another by the shoulders and with the direst expression on her face said, "If you want to survive the game, it is crucial that you hairspray the crotch of your panty hose before you put them on. I'm dead serious, your game is on the line." Clearly, her definition of *survival* and *dead serious* were quite different from mine.

Desperate to find something football related to put me back in the right frame of mind and with no football players in my locker room to help me get game ready, my playbook would have to do the trick. Though we had never cracked playbooks in training camp because our coaches insisted we learn everything on the field, I had requested a playbook. In the middle of the glitter, a camera two inches from my face, I pulled out the bright red Texas Revolution playbook. Whenever you're losing focus, the best thing to do is go back to your fundamentals. What are the nuts and bolts of your game? What's the mission of your position?

I opened the cover and read the offensive philosophy. I started to feel more confident and thankfully more connected to the game. I flipped through a few text pages, then got to the plays, but there was nothing actually drawn up. I flipped to the next page, and the next, and the next, all the way to the back of the book. The entire playbook was blank. So much for my fundamentals strategy.

I decided it was both far too loud and far too quiet in the locker room all at once. It was loud with everything but football talk. Up until this moment, I had said very little, probably because I was afraid I might say something wrong. Then I yelled, "It's too damn quiet in here. Can we get a little amped up? I need some music!" The dancers could not have been sweeter or any happier to oblige. I think they had actually been holding back on the music because they didn't want to bother me.

Suddenly, we all had something in common, and we all loosened up as the music blared.

"Now that we got that settled," I said, "I really need some help. This is crucial. Who can braid my hair?"

I warmed up to the dancers on that common ground—we were all getting ready to participate in a game we loved. But when I finally got to join my guys in the hallway, it was magical. Guys were getting worked on and taped up by trainers in the hallway. Some focused in moments of heavy concentration. All different, but all the same on game day. Every one of us on that team had something to prove that night.

In that hallway, with each high five, shoulder pat, or hug, though guys were playing for their individual futures with the team, they also made it clear they were playing with and even for me. The rest of the world was waiting to see what would happen when I got hit for the first time, but these guys had seen me get hit plenty of times. Shoot, most of these guys had personally hit me, and they knew I was tough.

To describe myself as one of the boys would not quite be accurate. In a way, they treated me like one of the guys, but in another way, I think they treated me better than one of the guys. It was like I was part of the crew, but I was also their girl. I think it was a point of pride that they were going to make history with their girl.

We grabbed our helmets, headed to the field, and lined up for the national anthem. With my hand to my heart, tears welled in my eyes, and yet before they could rush down my cheeks, the song ended. I quickly put my helmet on so my red eyes would not be quite so obvious, then high-fived the fans on the way to the bench.

Another player who had looked out for me since my first day, Javicz Jones, stopped me, put his helmet to mine, and said, "You've got this, and I've got you." I definitely didn't have the words to respond, but there wasn't time anyway. He quickly lined up for the opening kickoff, and I went off the field.

I don't think I ever made it to the bench. I was far too excited. I found a spot on the wall where I could elevate myself high enough to actually see, and I was soon cheering my voice out. (Literally, by the end of the night I had no voice.) It was like I pledged to myself that what I lacked in playing time I was going to make up for a hundredfold in cheering energy. Arena football is a fun, fast-paced game anyway, but I had never experienced it like this. I was a part of this team. These were my boys. I was not just on the sidelines but rather I was a part of these sidelines.

It was a weird situation. I was used to being one of the best women in the world. I was used to being that player who went in to dominate and make plays. Now, here I was on the bench, not getting in the game, and I wanted so desperately to get in, yet I also knew it was an honor to have made it to the bench.

The game against the North Texas Crunch was supposed to be a "tune-up" game, and yet I think the Revs were caught a little off guard when the Crunch came primed and ready. They were better than the Revs had expected them to be, and the Revs actually found themselves in a dogfight. I wanted to get in the game, but damn it. I knew they were not going to put me in while the game was tight. When we went into halftime, I still had not taken the field.

But we got a lift when we really needed it. The crowd had already picked up in both size and rowdiness. Then something extra crazy happened. Approximately 150 football players and coaches, there to compete in the first Women's World Football Games, rolled up. Women from nine different nations came to show suport. With those football-playing ladies in the building the energy and noise suddenly went off the charts.

I had felt their arrival, but I was still moved when one of my teammates said, "Welter, your girls are here." Damn right my girls were with me. The best part: not only did that energy lift the fans and me, it lifted the guys on the field, too. The team was electrified by the crowd's response. Several guys said, "Jen, don't worry, we're gonna knock these guys out. We have got to get you in this game." Despite very few strategy changes at halftime, the energy was completely different. The Texas Revs were a different team in the second half, and that team dominated the North Texas Crunch.

Finally, when my number was called and I ran onto the field, the entire stadium went wild. People were standing, screaming, and cheering. The international women's football section went absolutely nuts. I felt the energy and excitement deep inside my soul, but I could not give it my attention. As thrilling as the moment was, I had a job to do and an entire team of men on the opposing defense waiting to take my head off.

We got in the huddle, and the guys were amazing. They were serious, protective, and encouraging all at once. The quarterback, Josh Floyd, came in the huddle and called the play. Dive left. Xavier Stinson, another friend since day one, was lining up at fullback, and he just said, "Follow me. I've got you."

I took the handoff, saw the hole, hit it, and then I was blasted by two huge guys at once. Funny thing was, yeah, they were big, yes, it was a damn big hit, but I popped right back up on my feet. As soon as I was up, I heard the crowd erupt in cheers. *I had just officially made history*.

I expected the crowd to celebrate, but I had not expected to hear the guys on the opposing team celebrating my going down, and before I knew it, I was shouting back, "Is that all you've got!" I wasn't hurt, and I couldn't let them think I was intimidated.

The guys on my team heard me and were so proud. We lined back up in the huddle and this time it was dive right. I did not even have time to try to hit the hole. I was blasted immediately. I flew back what felt like ten feet and landed on the ground. The crowded gasped. And then paused.

But, though I had been hit hard, I was not hurt. I popped right back up. Again the crowd's gasp turned into screams of celebration.

LATER IN THE game, I was put back in again for a couple more plays, one of which involved a gorgeous fake handoff by Floyd that led to his scoring instead of me. I was thrilled we scored, but it turned into this strange moment in sports when the crowd both cheered and booed. They wanted a woman to score a touchdown. We had been one step away from that happening. Some of the guys even said that the fake was so good they thought I had the ball!

No touchdown ever came for me. Although my game consisted of three carries, three big hits, and a loss of one yard, I had gained respect. Still, judging by the pulse of the crowd, you would have thought I was the MVP.

COACH JEN: TEAM IS POWER

The openness of the Revolution guys to my joining the team is a testament to the power of teamwork. Team unity is one of the most powerful assets of any organization. It is taking a group of individuals and breaking past perceived differences and previous alliances, tapping into individual resources, and ultimately placing them in positions that maximize their contribution. The power of the group is greater than the sum of the individual parts. Creating buy-in around a common vision and common goal is the objective of every great leader. In football we say playing for the name on the front of the jersey is more important than playing for the name on the back.

Allies in Opposition

Sometimes, you have to handle the opposition on your own.

During pregame stretch at our first regular season game, I heard a player on the opposing team yell, "Dooooctor, Dooooctor! . . . Someone help me, I'm calling the doctor."

I ignored it.

"Ohhhh, is the doctor too good for me? Oh c'mon, dooooctor. You guys better protect her, cause if I get my shot I'm gonna hit the doctor," he taunted. "I'm gonna give her some extra, too, she's cuuuuute."

I didn't say anything, but I could see my teammates getting agitated and exchanging glances.

The guy making the noise was starting to get to them, and he knew it. He smelled blood in the water, so he amped up his attack.

"Ohhh, dooooctor, can you examine my head for me?"

I couldn't resist any longer. I blew him a kiss.

"Oh, doctor, I like you. They say I have mental problems, can you help?"

"They say I'm crazy for even being out here with you guys," I said. "So I guess we will get along just fine."

My guys were upset. They wanted to fight him.

But I got in their faces. "Don't you dare let him use me to get to you! If he gets in your head, I will kick your asses myself!"

Later in the game, I flipped the script.

The player who had been talking so much trash in warmups brushed past me after a play. I knew my guys were watching, and with the game just about to be won, I could not let them start a fight. I had to think fast.

I got in his face (well, more like his chest, given my height). I looked up at him and said, "Hey, did you just grab my ass?"

It was the last thing he ever thought he'd hear on a football field. The look on his face was absolutely freaking priceless. His eyes were wide and his head was drawn back, and then he turned toward the rest of the guys on the field and said, "Yo, the doctor just asked me if I grabbed her ass. Yo, you guys got a good one, she's cool. I love the doc."

My guys lost it laughing. Just like back in training camp, my team needed to know I could hold my own physically and with the mental jabs as well, and the opposition needed to know the same thing. The locker room handled itself, but some of the opposition

I had to handle myself. The fact that he never fazed me, that I actually smiled in the face of his aggression, and that I talked some smack along the way disarmed him and then charmed him. He became one of my most avid supporters.

The game was over, we had won, and I had scored major points, even though I didn't score a touchdown.

Going into the season, having a woman play men's professional football was a nightmare in the making for a number of reasons. Naturally, everyone had assumed the worst: outside the obvious physical risks, many of the critics assumed there was nothing I could bring to the team beyond PR. They underestimated me. The media saw a distraction, the opposing defenses saw a target. Thankfully the guys saw differently. They saw me as a teammate, and that was also a point of pride. Those guys responded in a way no one expected because we were a team, a team with attitude.

PLAYING ARENA FOOTBALL was the perfect preparation for stepping into coaching. I learned lessons the hard way. Because they were both physical and mental, the tests we went through brought us together. In coaching, the tests were very much the same, though thankfully no longer with physical contact involved. However, I cannot lie. The physical contact, the street cred I gained from actually playing football against men, was one of the things that helped me the most in my new position. By playing football with men, I transcended my own perceived limitations in the game. I want you, too, to learn how to tap into your best self in not just one area but all areas of your life. Let's refine and redefine what you are capable of.

CHALLENGE YOURSELF

Take some time to think about these questions and come up with some answers:

- Where is the place in this world that you are your best self?

- What is that thing that you do or that part of your spirit that elevates you to be your best self?

   Now, let me challenge you more:

- Can you single out that best part of you and make it part of everything you do in a day?

- Can you take the lessons you have learned and the feelings you have felt to be called upon in every area of your life?

I want little girls to grow up knowing that when they put their minds to something, when they work hard, they can do anything regardless of what the world defines as important.

|||||||||||||||||||||||||||||||||||||||||||||||||||||||||||||||||||||||||||||||||||||

9

When It's Us Against Them, We All Lose

Doing difficult things, such as playing football, requires toughness. Being tough eventually gets easy. But making the transition between being tough on the field and being an approachable person off the field isn't always so easy. The toughness that made me hard to handle on the field, sometimes made me hard to handle off the field. But there's a flip side: Though it's hard to shift gears, versatility is also an extremely powerful attribute. Coaching and being mentored in return can be extremely powerful tools in learning versatility and developing skills that you don't even know you have. Unfortunately, I often missed some of those opportunities in my career. Sometimes it was because I didn't know how to listen; other times, it was because no one was willing or able to coach me. I want to give you what I lacked, the ability to be better than I was. Allow yourself to be coachable and to seek out and find those willing to truly coach you, especially for the things you find most difficult to hear or be coached on. Humbling ourselves is uncomfortable, but we have to get uncomfortable sometimes to achieve greatness.

AFTER FINISHING MY season with the Texas Revolution, I struggled to come up with a plan for the future. There was a lot of internal and external pressure on me—everyone wanted to know what was next. I wanted to know, too. Would I go back to the Revolution? Would I play for another team in the IFL? Would I return to my female football family and join them on their quest to form the Texas Elite? Was it retirement time? My nerves, coupled with the outside noise to have an answer, well, it was all driving me a bit crazy.

So many questions swirled in my head, as did the worry that perhaps I should have done more with the opportunity with the Revs. Nothing was clear in my mind except the fact that there was no direct path to wherever I was destined to go. In fact, the path seemed littered with almosts, not quites, failures, and disappointments.

I could not help but think the hits I took playing men's pro football were much easier on me than the ones I kept getting socked with in life. Some days, I felt content with my plan to retire and build a business. In the quiet moments, however, my mind would go to the gridiron, to my love of the game, to the place where I had dedicated my life for the past fourteen years, and to the thoughts of playing again next season.

To say I was lost and indecisive would be an understatement. It seemed as if the whole world was saying that what I did was not good enough. Sure, I had survived a whole season of men's professional football and therefore had accomplished more than anyone thought was possible, but that was just one year. If I did two, then I would prove it was really real. The external doubt got into my head, too, and I wondered if maybe I was trying to prove it was real to myself as well.

I was struggling with my athlete identity, and the idea of retirement was causing a very deep and personal crisis. I was a trained mental health professional. I should have been prepared and known better. I had consulted with many football players who were experiencing career transition. I understood it before, but this was different, now that I was actually living it.

Coach Rose from the Texas Revs reached out to me about a football player, a young girl named Wynter Nunu. She was about ten years old and, because she was playing football with boys, she was in need of a mentor. She played running back and linebacker on his team, and she was his star. Of course, when Coach Rose asked if I would come out, see Nunu play, and give her a signed ball at halftime, I was honored to say yes.

It was a cold Saturday morning when I went out to see Nunu play. I stood sidelines watching the game, smiling to myself as I watched her make plays all over the field. This little girl was good, she was tough, and she had heart. Coach Rose was right, she was a little mini-me, and I was so glad he had brought me out.

Unfortunately, Nunu's game that day was cut way too short. She was ejected for kicking a boy. With her helmet still on and fingernails painted, she wiped the streaming tears off her face as she looked up at Coach Rose. I listened as he talked to her, just a few feet away, then Coach Rose said, "Go talk to Jen." Little Nunu's eyes became huge as she realized for the first time who the unknown woman was on the sidelines. I smiled as she came over.

"Hey, Nunu, do you know who I am?" Without words, eyes wide with excitement and a bit of fear, tears still streaming down her cheeks, she nodded. I continued. "You are such a great football player, I was having fun seeing you play. What happened?"

When I said she was a great player, her eyes lit up and a hint of a smile crept onto her face. "He was holding me and kicking me, so I kicked him back."

"Hmm, so the ref kicked you out?" A few more tears rolled down, and she nodded. "Okay, so why do you think he was holding you and kicking you?"

Little Nunu's face got very serious. "Because I'm a girl."

I smiled. "No, it's not because you are a girl." Her expression shifted from mad to confused. "It's because you are so good," I said, "and he was mad that he was getting beaten by a girl."

A huge smile took over her face. "Really?"

I smiled again. "Absolutely! If you were a girl out there who was bad, those boys would be happy to kick your butt. The reason they had to cheat was because that was the only way they could beat you!"

Little Nunu grinned. "So other players picked on you, cheated, and tried to get you out of the game?"

I laughed. "Yup, my whole career."

At halftime, I presented her with flowers and a signed Texas Revolution football.

"Never before in my life have I had a girl on my football team," Coach Rose said. "Now in one year I have two. My girls."

We both leaned in to hug the coach, who softened up, though he would never admit it. If Nunu and I could soften Coach Rose, we just might be able to change the world.

There is nothing quite like seeing the world through a child's eyes. There is a refreshing simplicity and purity that sometimes we lose as we get older. Nunu's perspective, her powerful love for the game, was a perfect reminder for me. As I spoke to her, Nunu knew I had dealt with the same behavior of men trying to cheat to beat me at any cost because I was so good. The insight I gave Nunu that day was to take it as an affirmation that when they were trying to cheat they were scared of her and what she could do, so the only way the boys could beat her was if they could find a way to get her out of the game. Smile, take the compliment, and know that you are winning.

I had gone to the game for Nunu, but it was just as impactful for me. Seeing her struggle play out in real time and in a real game was a tangible reminder of the overall struggle for women in sports and what so many of us had been fighting for. Thankfully,

Nunu was growing up in a world where she had women to look to. I owed it to her and all the other little girls to keep playing hard, especially when it was challenging.

It's so easy to get caught up in all the individual battles and the small stuff. It is so easy to get frustrated and distracted, and in those small battles, it is tempting to feel like you are all alone and on your own. Then the fights, the holds, the kicks—they feel personal, and it's hard to see past yourself. The trick is to see the bigger picture, the bigger message, even when it comes in a very little package, like a young girl.

COACH JEN: MENTORING HELPS THE MENTOR AND THE MENTEE

Those moments I was able to share with Nunu and girls like her gave me a glimmer of hope about my future. Remember, when you're lost or seeking a little validation in life, giving is sometimes the best fix. I couldn't quite see it at the time, and I didn't know whether there were more chapters in my football life, but mentoring others turned out to be the push that kept me going forward. Knowing you can make a difference in other people's lives as you struggle with your own big picture can often carry you through a difficult time.

Giving time and support to others is also a form of receiving: you receive confirmation that you're on the right path and that you have value.

You can give back leadership or be a female role model to fill a void you experienced when you were young. Draw on what you would have liked to have had in a mentor. It feels good to show other girls and women what is possible, especially when they're also doing something without a road map.

What Came Next

Later that year, as I continued to wrestle with decisions over my future, I attended an event featuring some of the Dallas Cowboys. A friend of mine was hosting it, so I knew a lot of people there—players, Cowboys supporters, and football people. At the time, I had been fielding questions about the future of my playing career in men's football, but the Revolution had given me no signals about my future with their team. Following the season, Coach Williams had left the team, and his absence left us with more questions than answers.

I ran into my Texas Revolution family as soon as I walked in the door to that Cowboys event. I was unaware some of my teammates from the team were going to be there. The NFL and indoor football players didn't usually run in the same circles.

After an hour or so at the party, I met former NFL player and coach Wendell Davis—the new head coach of the Revolution.

"I must admit, I noticed you as soon as you came in the room," he said. "I saw the way you interacted with people, and I immediately said to myself, 'who is she?' Then you really confused me, when I saw how all the Revolution players reacted to you. So I asked Coach Devin Wyman here, my defensive coordinator, who is the girl that all my guys love? And he told me, Coach, that's your running back."

Coach Wendell, Coach Devin, and I all sat down and chatted. Coach Wendell grilled me about football and the organization. Since so much time had passed, I assumed my time with the team had come to a close, and I didn't hold back. I gave him my honest and unfiltered opinion about what was good, what was bad, and what needed fixing. Maybe because of my honesty, we clicked.

The next day I was at the gym getting ready for a spin class when my phone lit up with Coach Wendell's name. I answered. He said that he and Devin had spoken nonstop about me the entire ride home and that I absolutely had to coach the Revolution next season.

I was stunned. This was something I had not even considered. "What? I might still play, and I've never coached before. You're going to throw me into coaching in men's professional football?" I thought he was crazy.

"The relationship with the guys—you can't teach that," he said. "I can teach you to coach football. Not many men are going to give you this opportunity. You are taking this damn job."

I laughed and promptly turned him down. No way I could coach men's professional football. We said good-bye and hung up.

COACH JEN: BARRIER CRACKING IS HARD WORK. BREAKING A BARRIER MEANS BREAKING THE RULES

- Accept genuine, unfiltered honesty—you will see it is refreshingly powerful.

- Step up to challenges and opportunities.

- Be willing to do the right thing, regardless of the cost.

- Progress takes time—be willing to do the work in the long term.

- You never know when your breakthrough will come.

- Ask questions: The answers you expect to be nos just might be yeses.

Coach Wendell Davis Would Not Be Refused

The next day, without my ever saying "yes" officially, Wendell informed me of my position with the team.

Here's what happened. After Coach Wendell and I spoke on the phone the first time, he happened to be at the Revolution office later that day when my name came up. The person he was speaking to seemed nervous at the mention of me. I'd fought for the guys off the field, just like they fought for me on the field, and that made me a wildcard, a bit of a troublemaker, and, yes, someone who made them nervous. When he saw how the front office responded to my mention, he realized I had turned the organization down, not him.

When he was told "Watch out for Jen Welter," he knew I was perfect for his coaching staff. He responded, "Watch out for her? You're going to have to watch out for her. I hired her. She's coaching for me." He decided that anybody who made them that nervous was exactly who he needed. He accepted the job on my behalf. I had not agreed to the job I did not believe I wanted or was even ready for. Then he called me and told me I was coaching for him.

He was right not to let me say no. I believe Coach Wendell saw something in me before I even saw it in myself.

The relationships I had formed with the guys made me appealing as a coach. You never really know the impact your actions will have down the line, and my experience shows that you never really know who is watching you and noticing your strengths. I had formed those connections without ever thinking that someone else would notice and act on them. And yet, Wendell had seen it, he'd seen *me,* and realized the value that I could add.

When he called to inform me that I was coaching for him, he also informed me that I couldn't quit, because then my narrative would be "there was a female football coach once, but she quit." Coach Wendell certainly had my number, and that's how he added me to his coaching staff. I was about to embark upon my second history-making moment with the Texas Revolution.

MY FIRST DAY as a coach for the Texas Revolution went very well. I was apprehensive going in. Though I was afraid some of the guys might have problems taking coaching from a woman, I found out one of the reasons that wasn't the case.

When we were leaving the field, a player named Fennel came up to me. "Hey, Coach, I wanted to tell you something. I played on the North Texas Crunch last year. You know that first play when you got hit by two guys?"

"How could I forget?" I said with a laugh.

"I was one of the guys who hit you," Fennel said, with a bit of apprehension. "I mean I hit you so hard, I thought I killed you. Then before I could even get up and look, you popped back up . . . and you talked shit. You said, 'Is that all you got?' I literally questioned my manhood, Coach. I thought, 'I don't know, is that all I've got?'"

Wow, I knew getting up was big, but I am not sure I realized how big.

"You earned the respect of every player on the field that night, and beyond. Trust me on that."

I nodded and he continued. "I made sure all the guys knew it, too, so they would respect you as a coach. I told them all that same story. We've got your back, Coach."

I knew then why the first practice went so well. I had street cred. Again, the way I'd acted in one situation set the stage for the next one, in ways I had never imagined. The guys already knew I had taken my hits to earn my spot on the coaching staff.

My Credibility Notes

Long before my handwritten notes to players became infamous in the NFL, I had another set of notes that were equally impactful. As a brand new coach with very little direction, I took notes on the plays for my linebackers the same way I had taken notes for myself as a player. They were nothing formal, just keys to the way I read the game and what used to help me as a player. At first, I used them in practice, where I guarded them closely and shared them only with my linebackers.

But as coaches quit and the coaching staff diminished, my responsibilities unofficially expanded to the defensive line. One day Robert Williams, our nose tackle and defensive captain, snatched the tight roll of papers from me and looked though the plays and tendencies drawn out in pink pen. After a thorough reading, he held them high over his head, well above my reach. "Coach Jen, why have you been holding out on us? When are you gonna give love to the D-line?"

Demario Dixon came over and took the notes, and looked at them while still keeping them far above my reach.

Finally, I relented. I took photos of the plays I had written and emailed them to Robert and Demario. "Happy?" I asked, as I typed the email there on the field.

"Nope," Robert replied. He called the entire defense over and announced, "Everyone give your email addresses to Coach Jen. She's got great notes."

COACH JEN: LET YOUR SCREWS LOOSE

Though Robert Williams was calm on the surface, a fire burned behind his eyes. Once, as I tried to coach him up to let that passion out—for the good of the team and because playing with tension can cause injuries—he looked me right in the eyes and said, "Coach, I can't. . . . I'm scared."

I pulled him closer to me, and I said, "Listen to me, I know I have seen more in you. Playing tight like that, you are going to get yourself hurt."

"How do I get it out of me and just play? I am so used to having to stay level headed. . . . Just need to get back to the beast I've always been."

"I'm gonna need you to get a little crazy. Time to let those screws loose."

He smiled at that. He got it: We were talking about freeing him from his own demons, the inner fears that were keeping him from playing free.

What about you? Look at where you are in your life now. Can you find a past situation that might be holding you back from the future of your dreams? Now is the time to forgive yourself and learn to have a short memory. You cannot focus on the future if you are living in the past.

On the field, no one could beat Williams except Williams. When he got into his head, he would overthink things and play tight. I know, because I'm the same way, and I bet you are, too, at times. So, rather than hold yourself back, get a little crazy and let the screws all the way loose. You'll be surprised just how great you are when you trust yourself and your abilities.

Though my notes were better than I thought they were, what made them so effective was the endorsement of Robert, the defensive captain. He set the tone that studying my notes was the expectation and that he would hold players accountable.

The locker room was handling itself again. I did not demand their attention or force my authority on the players. They stepped up and took it, and as they got better and better, they demanded more and more. My notes got more and more detailed and involved, and I was happy to share them.

Many people have asked how I commanded respect from the guys, as a player and later as a coach. The answer is simple: I didn't demand it, and I think this is a key point. They gave it to me. Now, they did not give me unearned respect, but what they did was give me the benefit of the doubt based on how seriously I took the game, how I studied each play, and how I genuinely wanted them to improve, and of course there was the street cred I hadn't even known I was building as a Revs player before I ever started coaching. They all knew my history in the game. Some of the players had been my teammates, some had been on opposing teams, but they all knew where I came from, what I had done in the game, and that I would never ask them to do anything I was not willing to do myself.

Though I had been thrown into a coaching position I never sought out and actually turned down initially, once there, I stepped up my game fast. As I have said many times, I never wanted to be the first and the last. I never wanted the narrative about me to be: *we had a girl once, but . . .*

Success isn't created in the spotlight. It's the work you do in the dark. When you finally get that breakout moment, you're ready to capitalize on it. The lights turn on and you shine. Own that moment.

||||||||||||||||||||||||||||||||||||||||||||||||||||||||||||||||||||||||||

10

Don't Hand Off Your Destiny, Step into It

> We all have defining moments in life. The turning points, the forks in the road, the times we choose how to get up after being knocked down and whether or not to step up to a challenge or step aside. Nobody's life is perfect, but your life is perfectly yours. You define the legacy you leave by the choices you make at those turning points. When in doubt, make the choice that lets you be 100 percent authentic. Stay true to yourself and you will step into your destiny.

AS PASSIVE AS I had been about accepting the coaching job, I was the complete opposite about landing my NFL job.

Toward the end of the season with the Revolution, there had been some shake-up. Wendell was out and Devin, who was a former New England Patriot, was in as head coach. Around that time, the NFL announced that Sarah Thomas would be the first full-time female ref in the game. That was huge news. In response to the announcement about Sarah, a reporter asked Coach Bruce Arians if he could ever envision a woman coaching in the NFL. His reply was, yes, if she makes the guys better, then she'd be hired.

Some people knew I had been coaching pro men, but it wasn't widely reported. After that presser about Sarah, on their sports radio show Les Shapiro and Woody Hayes were debating the notion of a female coach and followed up to talk with me about it.

When I mentioned the upcoming interview to Devin, he suggested we call Bruce Arians to inform him that, in fact, a woman was already coaching. He actually asked me if I had Bruce's number. I laughed. Why would I have Bruce's number and why would we call one of the thirty-two most powerful men in all of football and expect he'd take the call? Not hardly.

Later at home, though, I got to thinking about it. I couldn't shake off Devin's suggestion. I became curious enough to try. I got on my computer, dug around on the Cardinals website, and found a contact number.

Knowing that being a female athlete is a full-time hustle, and with forty-seven jobs, I got on the phone and created another one that day—that of Devin Wyman's assistant. Believe it or not, I got extremely bold and called the Arizona Cardinals on behalf of myself, as if I wasn't myself.

After a few transfers, I made my way to Bruce's assistant, Wesley. I explained that I was calling on behalf of former New England Patriot and current head coach of the Texas Revolution Devin Wyman and that Devin had asked me to reach out to Bruce about his comment about a female coaching in the NFL. I said Devin wanted to talk to Bruce about the fact that there was a woman on his staff coaching men in professional football.

Wesley was great. He said he believed Bruce would want to talk to Coach Wyman but that it was an insanely busy time with the draft just around the corner, so it would be a few weeks. Honestly, I thought I had been blown off. Still, I was incredibly proud that I had mustered up the nerve to try.

A couple of weeks later, I walked into practice one morning. We started at about five-thirty in the morning because most players had to get to day jobs. Devin was giddy and downright glowing. Sleepy and puzzled about his early-morning enthusiasm, I half listened as he said, "You will never guess who I talked to yesterday on the phone for about an hour."

"No idea, Coach," I said.

Turns out: Bruce Arians had called Devin. He'd heard about me, through Wesley, and wanted to know about the girl who was coaching. Bruce had asked if I loved the game. If I knew the game. About my degree in psychology. If the guys respected me. And the big question: Could I read the guys' eyes?

Most importantly, Bruce asked if I would consider the Bill Walsh Minority Coaching Fellowship. Devin had said, "If she doesn't, I'll kill her myself."

I had never even heard of this coaching fellowship, and it was somewhat unclear what the next steps were, but still I was blown away. I had to sit quietly with the secret of knowing I was in the mix for a coaching spot with the NFL. Even though nothing was concrete or offered in writing, the idea of what might happen was surreal.

Later, I connected with a fellow football coach and friend Dave Diaz-Infante. As we caught up, Dave also mentioned the fellowship, unaware I'd heard about it earlier. Though it was a coincidence, some say there are no coincidences, and I took it as confirmation that I was on the right path. Then Dave mentioned that he had interned with the Cardinals the season prior.

I couldn't help myself. I told him what had happened, and he was ecstatic. He told me he thought Bruce Arians would love me. He promised to put in a good word with Bruce for me.

Weeks later, the day before he would see Bruce, I nudged Dave to make that call.

When Dave mentioned me that next day, Bruce's response was, *I wanted to talk to that girl, but she never called me. Give her my number.* I immediately followed up with Bruce myself and was told to come to the Cardinals practice the following day.

No way. Pinch me. Bruce Arians had personally invited me to an OTA (organized team activity) for the Arizona Cardinals because he wanted to meet me. It seemed he was actually considering hiring me as an NFL coach.

COACH JEN: GO GET IT

You have to be willing to make change happen yourself. You have to ignore your fear of rejection. Nobody wants to get turned down—that's ugly. And scary. But if the upside is a win, focus on the potential of what could happen. If something doesn't happen exactly where you're standing, then step one inch to the left. Pivot when you need to. Whatever you originally strived for might happen, but it might reveal itself in a different way. The path might include a detour. The vision you have of success might be different from how you've imagined it. Your effort, whatever you have put in, might pay off elsewhere. But you have to try. A *no* means you are no worse off than before you took your shot.

On the sidelines of that NFL practice, my mind was blown. For a girl who had been told her entire life that she was too small, that she shouldn't be in football, I couldn't believe I was actually there. In my entire football career, for as long as I played, I never imagined I would be standing in that spot at that moment in time.

I was nervous, but the familiar sound of pads popping quickly turned those nerves into excitement. This was still my game, after all, no matter the level. Whenever you feel out of your element, go back to the fundamentals. Coach Arians greeted me as I walked to the side of the practice field. He cut right past titles and told me to call him BA. Bruce or Coach Arians was too formal.

He was hilarious and completely at ease. Everything I had heard about him was true. Within minutes, I felt like I had known him my entire life. It was easy to see why his players loved him. He was warm and cool and conversational and smart. We talked football and practice and the NFL and more.

At one point, he said, "Coach, do you realize I can only put these guys in pads fourteen days? How the f*&# am I supposed to build a football team when I can only put them in pads fourteen days?"

"Well, Coach, maybe you should get some of the guys from my arena team. I can promise they haven't been out of pads fourteen days, and frankly I don't think I was out of pads fourteen days my whole career."

"By the way," he said, with a bit of a twinkle in his eyes and a smirk, "I f*&#ing cuss."

Keeping eye contact, I smiled and said, "Good, it's f*&#ing football."

This was the game within the game. BA was testing me to see how I would react to rough language. Obviously, if a simple word could throw me off, there was no way I could work in that environment. If we were going to get into the trenches together, he needed to know that I could hold my own, and that the game came first: the important f-word was *football*. If the other f-word fazed me, there was no way I could handle all the challenges of being the first female coach in the NFL. Thankfully, he saw what he needed to see, and on the sidelines we connected on both f-words. He had to get to work, but we agreed to continue the conversation later in the day.

After practice, we caught up in the cafeteria, just the two of us.

"You know, Jen, I've been thinking a lot about this. One of the best coaches I ever met was at Hinds Community College, the receivers' coach, and her name was Dot Murphy." He looked me in the eye as we stood in the empty room. "The fact that it hasn't changed or gotten any better in all this time, it's not right. If we do this, it's going to cause quite a ruckus. But if you're willing to step into chaos with me, I think we can do something really special. We have a great team here. Our guys are high-character guys. Our coaching staff is diverse. We have more diversity than any other coaching staff in all of the NFL. This is the right team, the right coaching staff, these are the right players, and you are definitely the right woman."

He got up from the table and extended a hand to shake. "I don't know yet if I can make this happen. I have to get all the right yeses, but I want you to know it's in my heart to try." And he left it at that.

BRUCE ARIANS: IN HIS OWN WORDS

No risk it, no biscuit:

My advice when it comes to creating opportunity is usually: Go for it!

People need to break barriers. I don't want to get political, but we don't need to build walls, we need to break down the walls. I think people need opportunities when they're qualified. But still, opportunity needs to be there. So, break it down and get to it.

Trust your gut, and your inner circle:

Before I hired Dr. Jen Welter, I didn't ask any other head coaches their opinions or their advice about it. I just did it. I had a feeling that this was going to work out. When my feelings are that strong, they are usually right. And this hire was just something I wanted to do.

I did, however, speak to my wife, Chris, and my son, Jake. And they asked the tough questions, specifically: Do you know what a storm you're going to get? Do you know what you're getting into? Yeah, I knew it was going to be a media storm. We deal with media storms all the time. But, hiring Jen, that was a positive media storm, and something that I felt very passionate about. And to be able to break down that barrier, well, I thought it was my duty.

Remember your own experience and your ascent when you're considering making changes or creating opportunities for other people:

Put yourself in the shoes of those looking to you for an opportunity—how would you like to be treated? My decisions often go back to when I didn't get something I thought I deserved and also knowing that when I got the right opportunity, it was because someone stood up for me. Also, knowing that the rest of the time you have to achieve things, but you need help. I decided early in my career that when I got into position, I was always going to help.

When I got the job with the Cardinals, I had 423 emails and two-hundred-something calls from people looking for work. I returned them all, knowing that not one of them was going to get a job. But I felt that they needed reassurance that somebody actually heard their request and listened because I was in their situation nine or ten times, and a lot of people never, ever answered. But I really respected the ones who did.

Bruce Arian's Tips for Building a Diverse Team

- Make sure you hire teachers.

- You can't have eleven ideas people—you need only two or three.

- Everybody else has to be able to teach.

- Don't discriminate—not on age or ethnicity. Diversity creates a better pool of knowledge.

- In football, people go with height, weight, speed way too much, and not the love of the game. And how much they will run through a wall to play the game. But in every field, when you're assembling a team, look beyond the basics. I considered preparation, leadership, and communication in my team; it's easy to get caught up with the best athletes, but there has to be something more or it won't work out.

COACH JEN: UNFORESEEN GOALS

Certain initiatives, like graduating college, require long-term goals that you can break down into measurable increments of success: to graduate college, I'm going to take these courses in these semesters, pass those classes, and boom. It fits in a nice little box. But sometimes the box grows bigger than you planned. You thought it was going to be four years to finish, but that turns into five. You make adjustments step by step.

However, not every goal is clear-cut. I have had goals for which I've experienced the exact opposite, essentially a reverse model of goal setting. It's striving toward a vision that you don't know is even there—you know the purpose and direction are right but don't know what the end result will be. Sometimes that end result is the opposite of what you might have expected. Sometimes you have a vision and you just don't know the small steps to work toward it, you don't know what the journey looks like. In football, I promised myself I would step up to every challenge that presented itself, even if I wasn't sure where it would lead.

You can't plan for something you don't know is possible. So, in some situations, you can clearly define goals, and in others, you start with a vision and make a promise to keep advancing. Look at life as a journey toward refining who you are and what you love and where you're successful. Sometimes I tried this and it didn't work. I went in one direction, but I had no overall purpose, so I kept walking and working and taking opportunities that led me in another direction. Look for defining moments and then be willing to step up and take them.

Two weeks went by and I heard nothing more from BA. I was not quite sure what to do. I had to concentrate on winning a championship for my team, yet, almost daily, I revisited every word of my conversation with BA and remembered he had said to let him know how the championship quest was going. I was nervous to call him, but I figured because he had asked, I had an in. So I called.

I got him while he was golfing. I told him I just wanted to let him know that we had made it to the championship. I was floored by what came next. He congratulated me and then said it looked like that fellowship was going to happen for me.

"Go win that championship," he said as we hung up.

It was like a drive-by of good news and I had whiplash.

I asked myself, *Did that just happen? Am I on my way to the NFL?*

Yet again, a man in the ultimate boys' club had believed in me and bet on me. When there are no women, it can take a man to believe in you. For me, it took a man to help break the glass ceiling. It took a risk taker and someone who had also been overlooked his entire career to be willing to change the game. Dot Murphy and the impression she left on him years prior put the initial crack in that ceiling. If only she knew the impact she had all these years later.

I'm not going to lie: I was nervous and excited. I thought back to all the times I considered handing my opportunity off to someone seemingly more qualified—and to Odessa's words of encouragement. This time, I knew I was taking this job. I knew I would step up, and I knew it had meaning. It certainly wasn't the path I expected to be taking. It exceeded my expectations. But I realized in that moment that the paths we take often zig and zag before they arrive at what feels like destiny.

COACH JEN: DON'T HAND OFF YOUR DESTINY

You cannot hand off your destiny. You were made for something great, and your path is your path. Other people might not see it or understand. They'll often call you crazy for walking it. You may even think you're crazy for taking a path, but you have to own your brand of crazy and your journey. I always say, "I love my brand of crazy, and to other people it may not make sense, but it doesn't have to make sense to them. It has to make sense to me." Remember that nobody else has been given your unique skill set or opportunities, and that combination of personality, skills, and opportunities makes you who you are.

R efuse to live your life in the past. Your greatest accomplishment should always be your next one.

||||||||||||||||||||||||||||||||||||||||||||||||||||||||||||||||||||||||||||||||||

11

Go All-In

Focus on what you're good at. Be consistently good at it and exemplify that with your approach and efforts. Spend no time worrying about what people are going to think about you or how you tackle challenges. You can't control what people think. You can only control what you put into any given situation. So focus on the components of each situation—your process. That's what it takes to be successful.

GOING TO THE Arizona Cardinals was the opportunity of a lifetime. What I didn't know was what would happen after the third preseason game. I could be hired to stay on, or the gig could come to an end as per the contract we had in place.

I realized I had to go after this shot with no hesitation and no restrictions, and therefore I had to sell my condo in Dallas. I had to be free to go where I needed to go and to be able to afford to chase any opportunity as well. I had to be ready to make Arizona my new home long term if the opportunity presented itself.

For someone who had once lived out of her car, the thought of selling my place was terrifying. When I had finally gotten a place of my own, I made it truly special. I put so much time and energy into it. I was starting fresh, and I had very little money, so I invested my talents and time in that place to make it a home. Of course, I Venetian-plastered the walls in the downstairs living room, kitchen, and dining room and I painted every other wall and every cabinet. My home had truly become a work of art. It was a place I created to heal, and now it was time I let it go.

Selling was a risky play. I would be giving up my security and my safety net to chase this football dream that, yet again, had no guarantee.

Still, I bet on me. I jumped, hoping the net would form while I was in midair. Sometimes that's the only way.

COACH JEN: NO NET NEEDED

Sometimes, what you see as a safety net is actually holding you back. A net is only as good as its placement. Beneath you, it keeps you from falling; above you, it keeps you from spreading your wings and flying. What life would you lead if you had no fear of falling and no fear of flying? No restriction. Nothing and no one holding you back or holding you down. How high would you fly if you realized you had wings?

Before I went to Arizona, I spoke to Larry Foote on the Cardinals staff about ways in which I could prepare. He emailed me notes on things to learn about the team (the full playbook wouldn't be handed to me until I arrived). I had enough to study like crazy for that month.

Each team in the NFL, probably like any team in sport, has its own language. A lot of what I read about the Cardinals, I could translate because it made sense to me. But as I studied the pages

Larry had sent, the term *salt and pepper* kept coming up. The formations didn't look fundamentally different. I'd seen those my entire career. But I had no idea: What was this salt and pepper thing? Salt and pepper, I convinced myself, was common, important, and significant, not just for the Cardinals, but for all of football. I felt like I should have known, and because I didn't, I panicked. *Oh my gosh, I am way out of my league. How could I possibly not know what salt and pepper is?* I didn't want to call Larry and show my lack of basic knowledge of the game and risk revealing myself as inexperienced and stupid.

Because everything was confidential, I felt trapped with this question with no way to find the answer. But I came up with a plan to casually ask Devin about it one day when we met for lunch.

"Hey, Coach Dev," I asked at the table, "what can you tell me about salt and pepper?"

"Uh, Jen," he said, picking up a set of shakers, "they're spices that sometimes you add to your food. You know, to kick it up a notch, right? If it's a little bland, you add a little salt, you add a little pepper. Are we good?"

"Um, Coach, not really. I meant *salt and pepper* when, you know, we're talking about football."

He laughed. "What are you talking about? There's no salt and pepper in football."

"I got some of my stuff for the Cardinals, and I was studying. I thought maybe I am way out of my league because it talks about salt and pepper, and I have no idea what they are talking about. I thought maybe it was an NFL thing."

"Jen," he said with a smile, "you've got to remember that every team has its own language. The formations and plays might be the same, but how we describe them is very different. Don't worry about it. You'll learn about salt and pepper when you get there."

I was incredibly relieved. It was something so simple, yet I couldn't get past my first impression about it—that it was about my failure. I let it intimidate me.

Don't Question Yourself

Salt and pepper sticks with me big time.

Seriously, salt and pepper had the power to make me question fifteen years of experience in football, question the history I had made in the game. And then it reminded me that I wasn't lacking anything and that I would learn what needed to be learned. Worrying too much about what I lacked rather than what I brought to the table was counterproductive.

Coach Dev's words reminded me to tap into my confidence and choose it over insecurity. *Salt and pepper* was minor terminology—sometimes we waste too much time on the minor things and distract ourselves. Knowing it was okay not to know that tiny term liberated me from my fears. There are things we won't know in life, but they'll eventually reveal themselves. Questions are okay. Being confident is okay. Accepting that everyone does something differently is okay. Starting a new job and taking five minutes to learn the language—even if you've done that job well elsewhere for years—is okay. Learn the system. That's okay. Salt and pepper—it had me spinning for absolutely no reason, chipping at my confidence for no reason. Ultimately, I figured out what it was very quickly upon arrival.

COACH JEN: SIMPLE AS SALT AND PEPPER

I share the salt and pepper story because it is wonderful in its awkward simplicity. I had no doubts in the substance of football, the meat and potatoes of the sport, but the spices caused me to question my capabilities. I think everyone has those moments of doubt.

Can you think back to a situation when you asked a question and got an answer that helped you proceed with your task at hand?

Now think about a time when you hesitated, fearful that needing to ask a question meant you weren't enough—smart enough, prepared enough, educated enough.

Compare the outcomes. Was asking what you didn't know all that painful? Don't hesitate to admit that you don't have all of the answers. Being curious, asking questions, improving your understanding of a situation or task, those are all positives.

The takeaway here: figure out a way to humble yourself. Most of us have trained ourselves to stay in a safe, relatively judgment-free bubble where we spend our time focused on what we are good or great at. In the process, our ego gets so protective that we shy away from things we fear failing at.

Instead, own your failures, put your ego on a timeout, throw perfection out the window, challenge your comfort zone, and do something you think you will be terrible at. Fear of judgment from others and from ourselves keeps us trapped. Sometimes failures bring freedom.

You can't blaze a trail alone; otherwise, you get stuck in the woods.

|||||||||||||||||||||||||||||||||||||||||||||||||||||||||||||||||||||||||||||||||||||

12

Wearing the Big Red Shorts

> You don't change the game by doing what's always been done. Whenever you're creating change, you're also creating chaos. There's going to be a certain level of insanity, but you do not have to become insane in the process. It's not always going to be pretty, but at times, it will be pretty funny if you let it. Roll with the punches and, when possible, roll with laughter.

WHEN I WAS first with the Cardinals, some moments seemed ordinary as they were happening, but looking back they were the most magical of all.

In the Arizona Cardinals offices, assembled in a room around a giant conference table, a collection of football greats awaited the details about what the next six weeks of our lives would be like as a part of the Arizona Cardinals coaching staff.

The 2015 Bill Walsh Minority Coaching Fellows, lovingly referred to as the coaching interns, took turns around the table and introduced ourselves as we waited to meet with Bruce Arians. These guys were impressive. It was a mix of guys with impressive careers. As I listened to the introductions it was like a who's who of NFL royalty. It was a humbling experience.

In attendance:

- Willie Williams, cornerback, thirteen seasons, Pittsburgh Steelers and Seattle Seahawks

- Levon Kirkland, linebacker, eleven seasons, Pittsburgh Steelers, Seattle Seahawks, Philadelphia Eagles

- Rashied Davis, receiver, seven seasons, Chicago Bears, Detroit Lions

- Emile Michael Harry, receiver, seven seasons, Kansas City Chiefs, St. Louis Rams

- Rod Hood, cornerback, eight seasons, Philadelphia Eagles, Arizona Cardinals, St. Louis Rams, Tennessee Titans

- Keith McKenzie, defensive end, linebacker, nine seasons, Green Bay Packers, Cleveland Browns, Buffalo Bills, Chicago Bears

- David Kelly, receivers coach, Canadian Football League and college ball, including at University of Central Florida, University of Georgia, Louisiana State University, Stanford, and Georgia Tech

Needless to say, I was listening to all of these introductions and feeling intimidated.

And then it was my turn: Jen Welter, linebacker, fourteen seasons, Mass Mutiny, Dallas Dragons, Dallas Diamonds, Texas

Revolution, Team USA, with a master's in sport psychology and PhD in psychology.

I immediately heard, "Uh oh, there's a doctor in the house." The jokes that I was "overqualified" flowed. My intimidation melted away. We quickly fell into easy small talk as we awaited the more serious part of the day.

At one point the discussion turned to the tragic situation with the Giants, where Jason Pierre-Paul had injured his hand earlier that year with fireworks. He lost a finger and it put his career in jeopardy. One of the vets spoke up and said that back in the day nobody would have touched fireworks. As we sat there, these NFL veterans suggested that our first order of business should be writing up a manual outlining all of the things the players should not do, including using your hands to light fireworks. That point would be top of list, considering hands were an integral part of a football career. We were kidding, of course. Even though we weren't talking strategy or football, we were learning so much about each other through our casual conversation.

Soon enough, Coach Arians came in the room.

Bruce Arians is direct. He does not mince words or send mixed messages. What you see is what you get, and you better either get yourself together and get on his team or get out of his way. Period. He quickly let us know where we stood and set the expectations. "This might be an internship, but if you think that means you are holding a clipboard, you're in the wrong place. You're here to coach." That's how BA described our job with the team. BA was very clear in his positioning of us. Training camp had additional players, which meant the need for additional coaches. He established that footing on day one, and never were we referred to as interns or fellows, it was simply and clearly, "coach."

A few more words, an explanation of the general game plan, and he was out. We were encouraged to get to know the other coaches and explore before heading to the hotel.

After that meeting and the tour, I had a few minutes with BA and team president Michael Bidwill. I was informed then that they would hold a press conference to announce me as the first female coach in the NFL. No pressure there. The chaos BA had asked me to step into was under way.

In the Spotlight

Later that day, we all checked into our team hotel. In addition to normal stresses of reporting to camp, I had something else to worry about. Something I was fairly certain only I was concerned with that day. I looked at my hands and realized I was desperately in need of a manicure. Given the haste in which I packed up and made a run for Arizona, it wasn't a surprise that my nails were in tatters. Just because I was a football coach did not mean the state of my hands was okay. I couldn't be front and center of the press conference with horrible nails. I couldn't do it.

While most of the guys settled in at the hotel that would be our home for the next few weeks, I explored the open-air shopping plaza in search of a nail salon. Thankfully, I did not have to go alone. Fellow coach Emile joined me. We'd known each other for years. He used to train clients at the same gym as I did in Dallas. We hadn't seen each other in seven or so years.

I was glad to have a friend along and to have a chance to catch up with Emile before it all got crazy. We sat side by side in the big chairs, soaking, and I explained to the manicurist that I wanted a gel manicure and pedicure.

For years when I played football, my game day ritual was to go for a pedicure, to escape and study my plays. Today was different.

This was no relaxing pedicure. This was an image mission. The news was breaking that the Cardinals had hired the first female coach in NFL history. It was happening. Suddenly, my job was no longer a secret. As BA had predicted, the news caused quite a stir. My phone was going crazy. Word was catching on and even with both hands dedicated, I couldn't keep up with the explosion on my phone.

As I was reacting to the news, with no warning, the manicurist snatched one of my hands and started to aggressively chip away at my nails, perhaps unaware that my previous manicure was gel. It was agonizingly painful. I was dying and distracted, not to mention frustrated by the scene in general. And I couldn't use my hands to answer, scroll, and search the breaking news. I tried to coach her up nonverbally with gestures of filing my nails and soaking them, but she dismissed me and proceeded. Emile and I had to laugh. I was in pain while the world was hearing about the history I was making. Messages arrived rapid-fire on my phone and I was busy arguing with the lady hacking at my hands. I thought for certain I was being punked right then and there.

Finally, the manicurist walked away and returned with a bowl. She set it down and thrust my fingers into it. Suddenly, pain flared in my hand. It burned and stung terribly. I looked down and realized why: the bowl was on fire! The dish was filled with acetone that had caught fire from the burning candle on the table. I snatched my hand out and I looked like the Human Torch from the *Fantastic Four*. My entire hand was a shooting flame.

All I could think to say was, "Oh! You caught my hand on fire! You caught my hand on fire!" I should have been screaming, but I was in shock.

Fortunately, acetone burns quickly. How terrible it would have been to have burned my hand the night before a mega press conference announcing how I was breaking a barrier for women across the country and to have to explain that it was done while I was getting my nails polished.

Breaking News: First Female Coach Taken Out by Flaming Manicure

I couldn't help but flash back to that intern conference room conversation earlier that day: *Players should not only avoid fireworks but also watch out for dangerous manicurists.*

I was almost defeated before I even stepped out onto the NFL stage—taken out by a manicurist. I started to raise a fuss when I was presented with my tab at the nail salon, but, glad to finally have nice nails for my first day in the limelight, I let it slide, paid, and left, still in pain.

COACH JEN: LAUGHTER IS THERAPEUTIC

Ultimately, the hand-on-fire situation was just what I needed. It was perfect because Emile and I laughed about it for so long afterward. Back at the hotel I shared the experience with all the guys. The *manicure massacre*. That's what we called it. And it set the stage for how we'd handle things: with a lot of laughs. When in doubt, laugh it out.

Just like people, no situation is one size fits all. When you get into something new, there are sometimes growing pains. Take, for example, hiring the first female coach in the NFL. Obviously, people were concerned about the major things: would it work, would the guys listen, and so on. Other twists weren't as public, but definitely weren't anticipated ahead of time.

On my hotel bed was a box of coaching gear to wear, and inside the box were three pairs of khaki pants. Now, the equipment managers had asked for my size prior to training camp, but women's sizes are hard to predict, so to avoid uncomfortably tight pants, I erred on the side of larger. These khakis were way too large. So large that I could remove them without unbuttoning them. But even if they had fit, they still wouldn't have fit me. I couldn't coach football all buttoned up in khaki pants. The other coaches wore red mesh practice shorts. None of the guys had to coach in khakis, so I didn't want to either. I wanted the shorts.

I called down to the equipment room. I was told I was welcome to the red practice shorts, but they didn't come in my size. Go figure, not a lot of five-foot-two players or coaches with the Cardinals. No worries. I said give me the big red shorts. I didn't make an issue of it. I decided I would just rock the big red shorts. Honestly, I figured if the biggest problem from having a female coach in the NFL was big red shorts, then we were winning!

THE PRESS CONFERENCE was all about trailblazing and dreams coming true. I told that crowd of reporters that I could not have dreamed big enough to imagine this day could ever come. And that I didn't start playing football to be here. The beauty of it was that, although it wasn't a dream I could have ever imagined, now it was a dream other girls can grow up having.

Just before our press conference, the news of Brady and an update on Deflategate was released. In a later interview, there we were discussing both the first female coach of the NFL and Brady's balls. I have nothing but respect for Brady and wished him well, but I commented that I hoped we'd forget about Brady's balls long before we forgot that a girl was coaching in the NFL.

We can never take ourselves too seriously. We have to learn to roll with things. Laugh, laugh, and laugh. Everything is about perspective.

What if I had made the big red shorts an issue? That would've become a story and ultimately wouldn't have been good for my team. My point: you can't anticipate everything. You gotta wing it. Enter situations with humility and humor. That's one of the biggest keys to success in life. You can let those *gotchas* beat you. Turn them into great stories of those magic moments that weren't so magic.

Some people watching the press conference thought it was perfect and that I'd had great media coaching. In reality, I hadn't had any coaching. I was just honest and authentic. I just focused on talking about what I knew, what I could control: my own path, my own dreams, so that the distractions—my manicure, my wardrobe, Brady's balls—just didn't matter. That showed in how I presented myself. Focus on what you can control, and don't let the distractions deter you or detour your focus.

At a certain point, there are no more words. You are more than the words you have spoken and the words that have been spoken about you. If a picture is worth a thousand words, consider your actions priceless.

||||||||||||||||||||||||||||||||||||||||||||||||||||||||||||||||||||||||||||||||

13

Be Authentic as You Lead

> If you had the opportunity to step up, make a difference for someone, and change a life, a business, a sport, the course of history, would you be willing to do it? Would you be willing to step out in the midst of potential controversy and take someone's hand, take the heat, take on the status quo? Could you do it? What if I told .you, you will have the opportunities to change your life, the life of someone you love, the life of someone you have never met, or society as a whole? Now, hold tight to the power of proposed change and be willing to not just take that chance, but to set yourself up for success.

TIMING AND CIRCUMSTANCES are everything. The stars need to be aligned for me to make history.

When we first talked about the possibility of my joining the Arizona Cardinals, BA told me he was confident it was the right team, the right coaching staff, the right guys, and that I was the right woman to jump into the fray. I would add to that the right head coach, because without his leadership, to foster the involvement, engagement, and support from all of those parties, it would not have worked.

In the time since I left Arizona, I've thought quite a bit about why it worked, and why BA was exactly right, why he was leading the right team, and why I was the right woman, or I should say *the right long shot*. Understanding, from all angles, what it took to make history in football is a good case study in how to construct an environment that's conducive to change in other industries, too.

The Right Head Coach: Bruce Arians, the Visionary

It starts with Bruce Arians, and his willingness to embrace difference as strength.

A glimpse at his sidelines showed that BA believed talent is talent. I would venture to say BA and general manager Steve Keim pride themselves on discovering talent that other teams might have overlooked.

BA's career might have primed him to bet on the long shot because he had a tough road to his own head coaching position in the NFL. Bruce was the youngest head coach in major college football when he secured a position at Temple in 1983; he didn't become the head coach of the Arizona Cardinals until January 2013, which made him one of the oldest first-time NFL head coaches.

BA set the situation up for success before my first day on the job. This is key. If he did not have buy-in across the board, regardless of how good I was, it could have been a distraction to his team. When the stakes are as high as they are in the NFL, when everyone's careers are judged on wins and losses, there is no room for error. BA started by getting buy-in from the cleats on the ground—talking me up to the players to gauge their feelings on me coaching. Once they agreed, he continued getting approval from the top down.

After BA secured buy-in from the top, he then secured buy-in from the entire coaching staff. The next step was finding the perfect position for me to coach. BA chose to have me work with the inside linebackers as an assistant to Larry Foote. This was an important decision for a number of reasons. One: he was putting me in a position I was qualified to coach. Two: he believed Foote and I would work well together. Larry Foote was a young, hungry coach on the Cardinals staff. He had played for the Cardinals prior to an injury. Because he saw so much potential in Foote, BA kept him with the team by adding him to the coaching staff.

Foote took BA's play call and ran with it. He actively reached out, voiced his support, set expectations, and even gave me homework so I would be as prepared as possible when I walked in the door. Immediately, I could tell what BA had seen in Foote, and why he thought we would work well together. Larry Foote was a brilliant linebacker, one of the best to ever play the game, and he was also very Detroit, meaning he pulled no punches; there was no filter with Foote. He was a what-you-see-is-what-you-get guy, just like BA.

The Right Team: The Arizona Cardinals

In 1978, under the ownership of Bill Bidwill, the Arizona Cardinals hired Adele Harris as director of community relations. She was the first African American female executive in the NFL. Following in the footsteps of his father, Michael Bidwill continued the Cardinals' tradition of championing diversity by bringing me in as the first female coach.

The Right Coaching Staff: Diversity at Its Core

On the field, it is easy to see that football doesn't work if all the players look the same. Winning requires straight muscle, straight hustle, and every single variation in between. This same commitment to diversity is not always reflected on coaching staffs. However, the Arizona Cardinals coaching staff was already one of the most diverse coaching staffs in the league, long before they added a female to the roster.

The Right Players: Great Guys

BA enlisted the support of the players first. BA knew support from the players was key. He gave them a voice in the team's decisions. And created a wave of excitement throughout the team—the players knew the historical significance of having me there, and they were proud to be a part of the team leading the way and creating change in the NFL. Their enthusiasm and support were palpable internally as well as to the outside world watching.

Many of the players welcomed me and let me know they had checked out my game film. For athletes, checking out someone's game film is the ultimate sign of interest and respect. They had done their homework on me and knew about my entire football journey. They recognized that we had shared a struggle, that I was a player pushing to make it for so long, too.

Veteran players set the tone. Sean Witherspoon gave me the nickname "Dr. J," and BA even adopted the nickname, which he saw as a sign that the players had accepted me. Lorenzo Alexander, a super vet on the team, also established the mood for some of the rookies.

One day, when I was in the middle of explaining something to a rookie, Zo walked by. The rookie's attention naturally wandered to the special team's ace.

"Zo," the rookie said, "what do you think I need to do?"

"What you need to do is listen to Coach, because what she's telling you is exactly right."

On one of the first days in camp, with that vote of confidence and support, Zo helped solidify my credibility as a coach. He could have easily pulled the rookie away and taken him under his wing, undermining me. Instead, he helped establish me as an expert.

Again, the locker room handled itself.

Respect is an important standard to set, especially with young players. Playing then coaching arena football taught me to let the team leaders set the tone, to determine the locker room culture. It was much better for leaders to create the atmosphere and send a consistent message for the entire team to adopt than for me to "demand respect." Veterans can do it because younger players look to them for both guidance and approval. BA had brought in high-character guys. He had faith. And that allowed him to bring me in.

As leaders, we all face making historic change one day. Though his decision proved to be right, BA had taken a risk, and it could have gone all wrong. In hindsight, it's easy to say it was a logical decision and a smart move; however, the reality is, success was not guaranteed. Coach took a huge risk, and it could have tarnished his entire coaching legacy. There's a real reason everybody held their breath as I joined the team. BA needed buy-in all around to ensure there were no missteps. I could have been undermined, anything could have gone wrong. But I wasn't because Bruce had set the stage, and he was confident it was the right decision.

When you're in a similar game-changing situation, set people up for success. Create buy-in. Get everyone excited about the change you're about to present. Lay the groundwork. Talk to everyone. Don't surprise people or force a decision on them that is out of the ordinary. That's what BA did. Doing the work beforehand preempts issues. It whips up excitement. Give people ways that they can win as the result of a big decision or move. It will make a big difference.

Hiring me was a point of pride for the players—because Bruce did that work. They loved making history. They loved being a part of what happened. It wasn't just about me. If those guys didn't want to listen, they could have made my life an absolute hell. But they didn't, not once. They were amazing, and that demonstrated their leadership.

The Right Woman

Bruce believed I was the right woman to join his staff, and that was a huge sign of faith. I have thought a lot about why, and there are several reasons. Of course, my football career, both its length and my success, demonstrated I had a passion for the game and that I was an insider, so we could relate to each other. Having played with the Revolution and then gone on to coach gave me street cred. Add to that my degrees and the buy-in Bruce created, and he initiated the opportunity for success.

COACH JEN: STEPPING INTO A SITUATION. MY KEYS TO COACHING

- Disarm them to charm them.

- Allow players to come around in their own time.

- No prejudgment. Period.

- Be 100 percent authentic.

- Be the coach you always wanted; be personal. Beyond the x's and o's.

- Don't force it.

After the Stage Is Set:
Tactics for Making Your Mark

Now, let's be honest, no matter how amazing your new boss, your new colleagues, or the legacy of your organization, stepping into a new challenge isn't easy. Especially if you're the lone or first woman among men or you're thrown into an unfamiliar situation. My time with the Cardinals taught me a few failsafe strategies for effectively achieving what you want. New situations are going to be tough, there's no changing that. The "getting to know you" phase is difficult and awkward. My personal philosophy is to disarm them to charm them.

Disarm Them to Charm Them:
Show Your Lighter Side

First, no matter how aware you are of yourself, the situation, and the questions surrounding your introduction into that new team or gig, you will not be able to predict every potential uncomfortable "uh-oh" moment or fork in the road, and yet how you handle those moments sets the tone for the rest of your relationships. When these moments happen, use humor to disarm, to alleviate the tension, to allow for clarity. And then focus on your natural ability to roll with any situation by choosing humor over anger to naturally charm your colleagues or teammates.

When I played arena football, I learned quickly the two things the guys really needed to see: Did I belong? and Could I get along? With the Cardinals, I decided to provide the answers before being asked using, of course, my humor and my authenticity. The Arizona linebackers were a bit hesitant to joke with their new female coach, though.

One day, a veteran lightly tested the line, so I decided to take the bait and win them over. While we watched film in our meeting room, one of the linebackers made a sarcastic remark. I don't remember what it was, but I could tell he was dipping his toe in the water. I jumped out of my seat, leaned across the table on one hand, pointed at him with the other, and said in my most booming voice, "If you are going to go there with me, you better go all the way in. Don't half step with me. I have a doctorate in psychology. I mess with minds for a living, and I will own you, son."

Keep in mind, I never got loud, so this was out of character.

Finally, I cracked a smile to show I was messing with him, not seriously threatening. The room broke out in "daaaayuuumms" and "the doctor is in the house" and "get 'em, Dr. J."

I had answered the question—could Dr. J roll with sarcasm?—before it was asked.

"Any other questions, or can we move on to the next play?" Foote asked with a nod and a smile.

The guys needed to know they could joke with me. By watching my game film and through my coaching, they quickly learned that I belonged, but they needed to know that I could get along with them as well, that they could relax with me. After all, linebackers are the crazy ones, and if they lose that edge, they're lost. I never wanted the guys to lose their edge.

COACH JEN: GETTING REAL

There is nothing worse than walking on eggshells in the workplace. If you are tiptoeing around some real or perceived situation, things will always be awkward. There is no way to make progress if you can't get real. Take the awkward situations and address them head-on, and I promise, once you get past those, you will be well on your way to working together. When you are in tight quarters, whether it is a business, a family, or a team, you have to be willing to talk about things. Otherwise, you are creating a self-fulfilling prophecy: you won't work well together because you don't even know each other.

Our Cardinals inside linebackers group bonded first. I had answered their questions essentially before they asked them. Once we were all on the same page, I had to do the same with the rest of the team as well. On more than one occasion, my reactions had major impact.

In one instance, I was looking up at Markus Golden, coaching him up on something. As he looked down into my eyes, he nodded, and said, "Yes, ma'am." He immediately looked mortified, and said, "Coach. I'm sorry, Coach."

Never breaking eye contact, I smiled and said, "Markus, I will never get mad at you for good home training. You can call me ma'am. You can call me coach. You can call me doc. Just don't call me a bitch."

His eyes widened. "Coach Jen, I would never!"

"I know, that's exactly the point. We're good."

From that moment on, Markus and I were beyond good. No eggshells, no doubt, just a football player and a coach, regardless of title.

Disarm Them to Charm Them:
The Power of Laughter

You already know about my belief in the power of laughter from my flaming manicure story and, of course, the big red shorts. But really, it bears repeating. When people are unsure of how you're going to act or react, or what is or is not acceptable, there is inherent tension. Think about it. You know questions linger in a new situation. If you are the one who is new, many of the questions center around you.

But you have the power to cut through that tension, spare everyone from tiptoeing gingerly around, and shorten that awkward "dating period" by using humor to read their minds and clarify who you are.

COACH JEN:
A DISARMING LINE THAT ALWAYS WORKS

"You know you said that out loud, right?"

By dropping a quick hint like this, especially when it's a first offense, a potentially innocent mistake, when someone's said something pushing the edge of what's acceptable, you show that you heard it and you're not okay with it. But you're also not making it into a complicated issue. You might be giving the person the benefit of the doubt that they spoke innocently, but you're still subtly telling them to examine their words. It's an I'm-willing-to-give-you-a-chance line that lets them know they were out of line. You make that point, then you keep it moving on to the task at hand.

Disarm Them to Charm Them:
Be Authentic Above All

Training camp is the ultimate close quarters, when a team is essentially in its own little world, hyperfocused on preparing for the season, making roster decisions, and building camaraderie as a team. From the hotel to practice, to meetings, and to meals, training camp is designed to maximize the time by using the close quarters to minimize distractions and bring everyone together. There is no room for pretense and no room for awkward tension. It's a little like marriage. There are no secrets, so you better get comfortable.

With the Cardinals, Larry Foote really set the tone for the inside linebackers group. We had a work hard–play hard mentality. We got things done, with a mix of humor and attitude. With his Detroit-versus-everybody attitude, he led the charge through the get-to-know-you period, and we became a tight group. One day as we rode on golf carts, I thanked him. He stopped the cart, looked at me, and said, "That's okay, Jen, I'm gonna do you like I did my wife." I'm not going to lie: I was caught off guard. I had no idea where he was going with that one.

Foote proceeded to explain. "I treated her so good. I wined her and dined her and made her fall in love with me. Then when she was so in love, and so committed, that I knew she was not going anywhere, we were together, I pulled the sheets over her head, and I farted. I've got you, girl."

It seems silly, but that joke taught me something: once the guys became so comfortable that they would fart in front of me, I was officially part of the boys' club, and we were winning and coming together as a team.

To get to that comfort point, I stayed as authentic as possible. For example, there is a universal problem on football teams that could best be described as sideline creep. With so many players and coaches, it is hard to see the action on the field, so the natural tendency is for everyone to creep up next to the sideline. The problem is, as everyone creeps up, players and coaches cross the lines, and in game situations, this can translate into penalties.

Now, because every team has a similar problem to confront, a relatively universal solution is lovingly referred to as the Get Back coach. Simply put, this is the coach who walks the sidelines yelling "get back, get back." It is such a challenging job that it often requires input from multiple coaches.

Why am I telling you about the Get Back coach? Well, because my coaching style was to be very even keeled and not to yell. I had self-selected out of the Get Back job, but one day, two of the coaches, Brenson Buckner and Foote, were determined to get me to yell. They deemed me the Get Back coach for the day.

Game on. I accepted the challenge, turned to the guys, and quietly said, "Hey, guys, Buck and Foote are trying to make me yell. And I don't want to. Can you get back, please?"

To Buck and Foote's dismay, all but one of the guys complied. Woodley did not. Normally, yelling at Woodley caused him to step up in defiance, so his not stepping forward was already a win. However, I needed more, so I walked up, patted him on the shoulder pads, and asked sweetly, "Wood, can you back up for me, please?" Woodley responded with a huge smile, as if he was the star of a Colgate commercial, and said, "I'd be happy to, Coach." Then he took a dramatic, exaggerated step and put himself well behind the line. The coaches looked at him and said, "Really?"

Wood flashed that same brilliant smile. "She asked so nicely, Coach, how could I refuse? You should try it sometime."

Needless to say, that was my last day as the Get Back coach.

On the sidelines, the way the guys responded to me, playing along with the game, and stepping back to my simple ask, made a huge point. I did not have to yell to get their attention, and it was confirmation for me to remain authentic. I knew in my heart that yelling at the guys would have been not only inauthentic but also ineffective. Picture me at five-foot-two getting in the face—well, closer to the chest—of a six-foot-eight defensive lineman like Calais Campbell. I could jump my highest and still not be at eye level with him. Best-case scenario, he could completely ignore me. Worst-case, things got heated and turned into an argument. That was the last thing I wanted. Don't get me wrong. I held my ground and checked things when necessary, but I did it in my own way. Sometimes, when everyone else is yelling, the best way to be heard is to whisper.

Let Them Be Authentic

For the guys to be able to be authentic with me, and vice versa, was a major lesson that I brought in to the Cardinals experience. We had to develop an authentic relationship so that we relaxed around each other, let go of pretense, told jokes, established trust, let go of judgment, and ultimately came together around a common purpose. This is important in any team-building scenario, but this situation had an added dimension created by having one woman in the boys' club that allowed the men to step up.

When we were heading to Oakland and were about to walk up the stairs to the team flight, Rashied Davis (a fellow intern) put his hand on my suitcase and said, "I know how strong you are, but I am still not letting you carry your own suitcase." I knew exactly what he meant, and it was a welcome distinction. In so many ways I was one of the guys, yet he still wanted to respect me as a woman. I did not argue; why would I fight kindness?

Just because a woman is strong and capable, it doesn't have to signify the end of chivalry. Being in and succeeding in a male-dominated field does not mean you have to be or act like a man, and it doesn't mean the guys should feel like they have to treat you like a man, either.

We encourage people not to underestimate the capabilities of women, and I agree. However, we need to stop underestimating the capabilities of men in regard to women. Many people assumed that NFL players would not take to a female coach. This assumption seriously underestimated the caliber of the men I coached. My players stood up for me, and I will always stand up for them. Not only were they professionally receptive but they were personally invested as well. The very same players who embraced me as a coach lovingly introduced me to their moms.

Men like that step up to the opportunity to treat women with respect when the expectations are raised and leaders set the example that real men treat women well. I want to be clear that challenging men to be the best versions of themselves is not the same as dismissing bad behavior with the qualification that boys will be boys. I suppose that's why we say true tests separate the men from the boys.

Make It Personal

Another lesson I brought with me to the Cardinals team, and continued to learn while I worked with them, was to approach coach-athlete relationships holistically which meant balancing the player with the person. The players could read my résumé, check my game film, which established my street cred, prior to my walking in the door. Coaching is more than x's and o's: it's football knowledge and on-the-field experience. Beyond that, Bruce was right, players want to improve, and if you can make them better, they will listen. Players gave me their respect by listening to what I had to say and then incorporating my words into their game and encouraging others to listen as well.

In this situation, every player was fighting for survival, his performance under constant scrutiny. Personal connections and my investment in them as people as well as players became even more important. They embraced me as a member of their football family, and so did their off-the-field families. There is nothing quite as moving as being asked to meet the parent, wife, sibling, or girlfriend of one of my players. So often I heard, "Coach Jen, my mom is a big fan of yours, and she wants to meet you."

My response was always, "I would love to meet your mom. Let's do it right now."

The introductions usually went something like this: I greeted a momma or an auntie with a big hug, and as she tried to tell me she was a fan, I would interrupt her and say, "Momma, don't you dare. I am a fan of yours because your son makes it an absolute pleasure to come to work each day. In a most challenging situation, in what could've been an absolute nightmare if the guys wanted it to be, your son is amazing and he has embraced me as his coach. Momma, that is because of you. He is the man he is because of how you raised him."

Tears always followed. Those were special connections.

"Coach Jen, I've never seen my mom cry before."

"That's because her blessings are running over. You are her greatest accomplishment, and you make her so proud she can't contain her tears of joy."

People thought men in the NFL would resist being coached by a woman, yet with each introduction to these significant women, something became very clear: most of the guys had been coached by women their whole lives. When they allowed me to connect to them personally as people, not just as players, that strengthened our relationships both on and off the field.

COACH JEN:
KNOWING PEOPLE AS PEOPLE, NOT PERFORMERS

Barring a physical change, when an athlete's performance varies from one day to the next, the difference is often mental. Something is throwing off that person's game. This is called being human. Athletes are not robots. Even the best athlete is affected by life beyond the game. As a coach, this is a key aspect to understand about performance—knowing the human variables that influence your athletes.

This point is not restricted to the field of sports: this is life and we are not robots. We are real humans with real lives, and great leaders recognize that. Great leaders make personal connections that lead to success for all. Take the time to meet and greet the people who are important to your people, and show genuine interest when you do. A lot of the traits that you might respect in your colleagues or partners likely derived from their families. Invest in the person who taught them the life lessons that you respect so much.

Let the Situation Coach You

Later, after camp had ended, Cardinals player Kevin Minter and I sat around talking along with a friend of mine.

"What did you think having a woman there would be like?" my friend asked Kevin. "What did everyone talk about or what were they concerned about?"

Some of the concerns I had heard before, but one I hadn't. It wasn't about my gender but about how new coaches usually try too hard. They try to prove themselves and have something to say all the time to prove their relevance. The players wondered: Would I overcoach?

"You know," Kev said, "she never did that. It was very relaxed and easy, and she would just jump in where she could help, but it wasn't like she had to say something at every moment."

Be good where you're good and add where you can add. But don't overtalk. Don't overcoach. Helping people is in fact getting to know them and getting to know what they need.

Partly, this means metaphorically falling and letting the net form, letting the situation coach you. Let a situation set the tone rather than demand it be set your way. Work with the system the best you can from within instead of against it, and institute changes slowly, as you're coached to do. That way, you gain trust and develop credibility in a very natural way.

COACH JEN: DEVELOPING A GAME PLAN

The eye in the sky doesn't lie. This is a key phrase in football. It means that the game film always tells the truth. Film is objective. It shows what happened in the game—right or wrong. We review the tape and we adjust accordingly. We watch the film before critiquing players. We show them film to coach them on ways we can do better. The film is not personal. It has no opinion.

In your role, whether you're coming in to a new situation or looking to improve where you are, assess the field first, then develop a game plan. As coaches, we don't talk about a team, then watch film to confirm what we've already decided. We study the film, noting the design and the approach, and we explain that to our players.

To many people, silence is simply a killer, so they work extra hard to fill it to prove they are good and know what they are doing. I took a different approach. I decided first I'm going to listen. Listen, rather than talk, and assess where and how I can help. After that, I'm going to act.

Perception

Dr. Arthur VanLear teaches a communications class at the University of Connecticut. He plays a video of a female football player, who introduces herself, says she plays football, lists her stats, then proceeds to say her reason for playing football is so that she gets to hit people and not go to jail.

The professor then opens a discussion about what type of person she is. As you might imagine, students comment that she probably spends a lot of time in and out of jail, that she's aggressive, violent, uneducated, rebellious, dangerous, and criminal.

Finally, the professor reveals the truth. Perception and reality are often very different. "That football player you were discussing is actually my niece. She has a PhD in psychology and, no, she has never been to jail."

The professor is my uncle, and I'm the girl in the video.

I bring this up to make a point about perception and preconceived notions. We're often far too quick to judge on the basis of limited interactions with another person. Many people say that I focus on the personal aspects of coaching because I'm a woman, but that is a very limiting statement. My coaching style is not a male-versus-female thing, just like no coaching style is distinctly a 100 percent man or 100 percent woman thing. We need to remember this in every arena. Style and skill transcend gender.

Don't Prejudge

My focus on connections and interpersonal dynamics are more about empathy, pure and simple. I was accustomed to people underestimating me, undervaluing me, stereotyping me, and assuming that how I played on the football field defined who I was in life. The more I heard it over the years, the firmer my beliefs were that the stereotypes associated with football players were wrong—and I was determined to make sure my Cardinals players knew that, too.

No feeling is more constricting than feeling prejudged, as if you are condemned to wear an inescapable label. I promised myself, and every player I ever coached, "If I can help you, I will help you. In the game of football, and in the game of life. I will never prejudge you. Period."

Going in, I didn't know them and they didn't know me. So, rather than expect them to respect me because my title was *coach* and they were *my* players, I wanted to get to know them and let them get to know me. Of course, we all knew about each other, but there is a big difference between knowing about someone and actually knowing that person.

Don't prejudge. Don't allow yourself to be influenced by the prejudgments of others. Make your reality known, just like I did, on and off the field. My coaching game wasn't all *x*'s and *o*'s. It involved connecting in the hallways postpractice, asking questions, and getting to know the guys as full, multifaceted people.

Don't Force It

Training camp is the ultimate survival of the fittest situation. These guys had shown up in Arizona, along with me, to fight for their dream to play in the NFL. Ninety guys were invited to training camp, but only fifty-three made the final roster. As much as teams had come together, it is also common knowledge that not everyone will be there at the end of camp.

Going in, I was the ultimate long shot with the Cardinals, but it was also the shot of a lifetime, so I chose to adopt my philosophy from the football field and play every down like it was my last. I could not go in looking for a backup plan or protecting my heart from getting hurt by never fully investing and falling in love. However, this was my first time, and for some of the players, previous camp cuts had cut into their hearts as players, so their protection mechanism had kicked in: do not get too attached because then you can't get too hurt. You can't force people to come around to your timeline of acceptance. All you can do is be open when they do.

COACH JEN: AUTHENTIC LEADERSHIP

First, identify your strengths and weaknesses. Then, maximize your strengths; work on your weaknesses. Once you know your skills, use them to figure out how you might lead.

Accept that there are many types of leaders, and figure out which type you are. Make sure you also know your team, not just their skill set but who they are as people.

Some of my most precious memories from my time with the Cardinals are the ones that are the least polished. It was the comfort, the grind of training camp, the feeling of being in the trenches together. Knowing that it was rough, that we were all rough, that we were all fighting together, farting together, sharing the hustle, living the experience, and getting to know each other so that the team became stronger. Individual players and coaches put their differences aside and joined together around a common goal and became a football family.

I knew I might have quit on myself, but not ever on my team. Never on my players. That's leadership. Leadership is putting yourself at the back of the line, not the front.

||||||||||||||||||||||||||||||||||||||||||||||||||||||||||||||||||||||||||||||||||||

14

Leaving a Legacy

I knew the rules going in. I had a start date and an end date. The shot of a lifetime came with a limited window of opportunity for me and every other intern. The job that was far beyond any dream I had ever dared to dream was never intended to be happily ever after. They say that even for the best football coach, the coaching life is characterized as a life on skates, skating from one staff to the next. I knew the reality of the situation as it stood, but I had no choice but to give up my stability and go after the dream with no fear and nothing to fall back on. I laced up my skates and went after it.

TRAINING CAMP WAS essentially a wrap, with just one practice left that afternoon, then we would pack up everything, leave the hotel, and head to Oakland for the third preseason game. As I was leaving our morning walkthrough, the director of media asked me to address the media after practice that day. I didn't think much of it and agreed.

As I did most days, I used my lunch break to hit the gym for my work-and-workout combo. The gym was normally a hotspot, full of people. Usually, the general manager, Steve Keim, and I had our walk-and-talk or work-and-workout sessions in that gym. This day, it was empty. I was alone.

I studied plays while I got some cardio in on the elliptical. My phone buzzed and I grabbed it to see what was happening. A Twitter alert popped up on-screen—I had been mentioned in the news. It said something like, *though Bruce Arians would love to keep Jen Welter and other interns, there wasn't room on the team.* The words stopped my momentum. I got off the machine to catch my breath, not from the workout but from the revelation.

Now I knew why I would be addressing the media after practice. My historic run was not to be extended beyond *first female coach* to *first full-time female coach.* No miracle was going to happen. No miracle was going to change things.

A wave of emotions quickly washed over me. I couldn't get a handle on the situation—that I had been given this tremendous opportunity to coach here, that I had cracked open a door for women and the league and myself after a lifetime of playing for something bigger, and that it was over.

There *Is* Crying in Football

I refused to let anyone see me break down, so I wiped the combination of tears and sweat from my face, threw a towel over my head, and went up to my hotel room, careful not to make eye contact with anyone. Once safely in my room, I cried with a mix of pride for my accomplishment and sadness for the end of what I had been doing and would potentially not do again. And I cried for all of us who have struggled and stuck to a dream, despite the darkness.

I don't usually like to cry in front of people, but, if you're going to cry, cry. I say that knowing that everything you do and say leaves an impression. So, know and own what that impression ends up being.

That day, I cried tears of joy for those who would walk through the door behind me. I accept that it was a vulnerable thing to do—to cry—but it felt perfectly 100 percent okay in the moment. It was a release of all that overwhelmed me about the greatness and ending to my history-making NFL experience. It represented the single best way to discharge the weeks of excitement, accomplishment, thrills, and sadness of the experience.

Those tears were about so many things: the fact that I loved those guys and didn't want to leave and that the experience had been so great that I would have loved if it continued forever. But it didn't. Even knowing exactly what I know now, I would do the exact same thing I did then. A thousand times over, if you asked me. I would absolutely take that shot again, and every single time. I would go into it 1,000 percent, hoping I could create an outcome where I stayed on. The tears showed me it meant something. If I wasn't upset, if it didn't matter enough for me to cry, if I wasn't studying plays right to the very end, then it wouldn't have been so special.

Though I might have liked to stay in my room and hide for a while, there was no time. I had to be back on the field. I also had to address the press later, which meant, unlike anybody else returning to the field, I had to scramble to fix my makeup, get my game face on, and get back downstairs.

As I armed myself with what felt like my war paint, I made myself a promise. I would not let anything steal the joy from my last practice or my last few days. I would take in every last second and enjoy them all. Soak up all the minutes left in my NFL experience.

I've thought a lot about why I cried that day at the end of training camp, in that moment, as the end became real. It was a difficult truth, sure, but it was a private moment. The magnitude of the accomplishment contributed to my emotion, not just the sadness of its being over. The opportunity had been so good I never wanted it to end. But the tears also marked the difference between what it meant for me personally versus for the game as a whole and for all of the women who wanted to be a part of that game.

COACH JEN:
FIND THE PERFECT IN EVERY STRUGGLE

- Play each down as if it were your last.

- Look for the opening at each closing.

- You will never regret the work that you did, but if you don't give everything you will always question what would've been possible.

- Own your story.

- Just because it wasn't happily ever after doesn't mean it wasn't exactly the right decision.

After the last practice, I headed toward the big hallway to the locker room. There was a Cardinals step-and-repeat where these sorts of interviews were usually conducted with players and coaches. As I made my way there, I was surrounded by press, microphones, and cameras everywhere. They asked me to step up on a box so everyone could get a shot of me and so I wouldn't be swallowed up by the crowd of reporters.

As they pressed in on me and I answered their questions about the overall experience and how I felt walking away, I realized that perhaps throughout the preseason everyone had been waiting for a big "uh-oh" moment, the big screwup that letting a woman in man's territory would inevitably bring. As the reporters pressed for answers, standing on that box, I realized since the moment the news had gotten out that a woman was coaching in the NFL, everyone was waiting for confirmation that it was actually a bad idea. Failure and chaos were expected, but no "uh-oh" moment ever came. We were flawless. We never gave the critics any ammunition to say, "The Cardinals made a mistake by hiring the first female coach," or "See? This is why a woman cannot coach in the NFL." It simply never happened. We did the impossible, and we did it well.

A Perfect Ending

I was proud of how I handled the press, perched on a pedestal to give me some height, surrounded by a sea of cameras and a surge of microphones pressing for a sound bite. They never saw me crack. I held it together. I didn't realize one more important interview remained.

Later, I sat down with Lindsay Czarniak of ESPN. That big group of reporters wasn't really my scene, but this intimate setting was. After we chatted for a few moments, she pulled out the note I had written to Kevin Minter and asked me to read it on camera. As I read the words, I fought back tears.

When I finished the interview, Kev texted me. *Coach, make sure you get my note back. I am keeping that forever.*

THE NEXT DAY we flew to Oakland for our third preseason game, my first and only away game, and my last game with the Cardinals. That night was my last night, and once again I found myself up all night writing notes. But on this particular night, I upped my game a bit.

I had racked my brain for something special I could do for my players. I wanted to give them something from me, something unique that would be important and have an impact. Earlier I had ventured out shopping in Oakland, but nothing felt right. I returned from my trip empty-handed. There was certainly nothing I could afford to buy these guys that they couldn't buy themselves.

Finally, it hit me. I didn't want to buy them something, I wanted to give them something, and I could give them something that money couldn't buy: the realization that their value was greater than what anyone could ever afford to pay them. They were priceless. All my linebackers knew about my $12 check and that the most I had ever made playing football as a woman was $1 per game. I walked into a convenience store and asked them to make change. I needed a crisp stack of $1 bills.

Alone in my hotel room in Oakland, I transformed each dollar bill into a gift. On the top left corner, I wrote the linebacker's name. On the top right corner, I wrote *play priceless*. On the bottom left corner, in red, I wrote *heartbeat,* and in the bottom right corner, I signed it, then printed *Dr. J.*

I placed each dollar inside a card in which I'd written a few more important takeaways and memories I hoped they would keep with them long after I was gone. I wanted to leave them with the most valuable lesson I had learned in my career: when you can play beyond money, when no one owns you or defines your worth by a dollar amount, then you are truly free. Then you *PLAY PRICELESS*.

In the heart of Raiders territory, in foreign locker rooms, notes awaited my players. Those notes had once been such a departure from the norm, they had become national news. Now, the notes were an expected and welcomed part of their pregame routine. We had created a new normal. No reporters were given those dollar bills; in fact, most were kept private. Some of the guys framed them, and others safeguarded them in their wallets. Regardless, I know that from that moment none of my linebackers ever looked at a dollar the same way again.

Final Game Wrap-Up

It was a beautiful, sunny Oakland day, and as I threw the ball with my coaching partner in crime, a true mentor, I couldn't help but smile. Foote called me over. "Girl, stop smiling. This is the Black Hole. You've got to be hard in the Black Hole. Game face. We are linebackers."

I backed up and we resumed throwing the ball. As hard as I tried, as much as I tried to put on my game face, I couldn't keep from smiling. I was a football coach for the Arizona Cardinals in the National Football League throwing a football in the legendary Black Hole. It was larger than life, a reality bigger than I had ever imagined. The girl who was never supposed to be in football.

I was exactly where I was meant to be, and I was happy. One of the best chapters of my life was wrapping up with a perfect day. From then on, it was a blur. Before I knew it, the veterans had been pulled from the game, retired their cleats for the night, and changed into sneakers—the universal sign that a player was not going back in the game. As I saw the sneakers appear, I knew it was over.

In sneakers, Patrick Peterson came over to me. "Coach Jen, is this really your last day?"

Without the strength to say words, for fear that I would not be able to simultaneously hold back tears, I just looked up into his kind brown eyes and nodded.

He put his hand on my shoulder. "I heard so many rumors that we were keeping you. I never imagined we would actually let you go. I want you to know, it's been amazing."

Only Positive Vibes for the Woman on the Field

The experience was as close to perfect as could be, from start to finish. And the best part about it all: I was leaving the door open. My legacy on that field would allow other women to have that same opportunity. Big picture: that was the most important part of all of this. My job on the field was complete and I'd delivered what was expected of me.

Even though I was the person who accepted the job, I was never alone doing it. The spirit of all the women I'd played with was pulling for me the entire time, as soon as I'd taken the field with the Revolution to that last game with the Cardinals, and beyond, too. That's what gave me the confidence to accept the post and to know there was more to come for me and, most importantly, for all of us. Every effort, every call, every hit, and every moment I coached my guys up—with every note card, every everything—was about our collective love of the game and pushing it forward for women, not just about me. It was about opening that door . . . or kicking it down and playing for something bigger than yourself, something that cannot be undone.

We all need to do that.

A FEW WEEKS later, the Arizona Cardinals had their first regular season game. Though I was no longer a coach for the team, I had promised my guys that no matter where I was physically, I would always be there for them.

To that end, I left notes in their lockers. But, this time, I would leave not only notes for my linebackers but also something for all the players and coaches. These were special notes. When I had visited my sister and her family in Rhode Island, I was enchanted by the beautiful work my brother-in-law, Esteban Martinez, did with Zen calligraphy. He made a limited edition print, personally stamped and numbered each one, then I signed and personalized each one on the back. I had the notes with a Zen twist delivered to the equipment guys to be placed in the lockers, one last time.

The front read: *SOKU KON MOKU ZEN*

Translation: *Right Now, Before Your Eyes*

The back read:

I have always believed that if you truly live in the moment and focus completely on being in the play that you are in, then no matter what happens, you cannot be beaten. Life is not about the last play, or the next play, but rather this play, and this moment. If you look too far forward or look back, you miss the beauty and the power of right now.

I urge you to always go all-in. Play each down as if it were your last, and if each one of you does this there is no limit to how high this team of Cardinals can soar!

Play Beyond expectations. Play Priceless. Play Big.

COACH JEN:
ALWAYS LEAVE THE DOOR OPEN BEHIND YOU

- Be a catalyst, a spark, an instigator. Be a fearless, passionate, insanely dedicated power player who inspires those who come next.

- Let history hold you accountable. I wanted to do a good job and not quit because I was working in the spotlight. Even when you're not in the spotlight, act like you are.

- Embrace your life and realize your power to create a legacy.

- Whether there are a million people watching or none at all, your actions have ramifications. Know that your existence in the world does not stop and end with just you.

- There's always something bigger to consider—and always somebody up next.

Football, Family, and Faith

"Football, family, and faith," is a saying we use to capture the idea of playing for something bigger than oneself. We're not in this big world alone, as individuals. We're not playing by ourselves. Think about my coaching and playing with men. If it was just me and nobody was watching, would I have been brave enough to take those hits? If I didn't believe in something bigger, would I have risked everything? No. But knowing that I was doing something for all the girls and women who've loved football for a very long time? Absolutely.

To this day, it is still those women I played alongside who drive me to keep pushing forward. They remind me that the hustle is real, and the struggle is ongoing, and my part of the story is only one chapter, neither the first nor the last as a football player or coach. Women were documented playing organized football as early as 1896. In 1967, the USA (or Cleveland) Daredevils, an all-women's team, was formed to challenge men's semipro teams and they played three games. The Daredevils provided the anchor for the birth of the 1968 plans for the WPFL, which was established with four teams in 1971.

Though one part of the story closes, the book's not over. What we did in Arizona was a beginning for women in the NFL, such as Kathryn Smith, who was hired by the Buffalo Bills. I wish I had been hired as the first full-time female coach. However, knowing that Rex Ryan called Bruce Arians prior to hiring Kathryn is the ultimate confirmation that we started something very special in Arizona.

It is so amazing to see how the game is changing, thanks to Bruce Arians and his willingness to step out and be different. When he was asked if he thought my hiring was an effort by the NFL to clean up its image with women, he replied, "The NFL had nothing to do with this. It was me and her." What a beautiful, simple truth. This was not a forced change or a response to a mandate. It was the right thing to do done by the right coach, who extended an opportunity to the right woman, with the right team, as a part of the right coaching staff, working with the right players. And it changed the game.

Change always needs a catalyst, and something very special has happened in the NFL. The league committed to developing a pipeline to increase opportunities for women on the football field, and it hired longtime women's football advocate Sam Rappaport to lead the charge. The Atlanta Falcons also gave my Team USA sister Katie Sowers a full-time position after she participated in the Bill Walsh Diversity Coaching Fellowship. Yes, the Bill

Walsh Minority Coaching Fellowship was changed to the Diversity Coaching Fellowship. Women aren't technically minorities in the population, but we are in football. It was a small tweak, but a meaningful one. There always has to be a first, and I'm moved to think that my experience might in some small way allow for more change to come.

The beauty of team sports is that your impact on the outcome is far bigger than your contribution on the stats sheet. Your energy affects your teammates as well.

||||||||||||||||||||||||||||||||||||||||||||||||||||||||||||||||||||||||||||||||||

15

A League of Our Own

> Be the heartbeat in everything you do and realize that your energy is contagious. The true impression a player makes is not simply captured in the plays. Those moments in between the plays can be just as powerful. In every play you make and in every huddle you break, you better own it. Make a statement. Leave no doubt that you belong on the field and in the game. Own your impact!

WHY DOES IT take playing a man's game to open up the same game to women? Why is it the ultimate goal for a woman to compete against men in sports? Why can't women compete against women without is requiring them to be willing to play for $1 a game? There is a fine line between nobility and novelty. It is noble to play for something bigger and a belief in the future, but at some point, the impact is reduced to being a tolerated novelty, and it sends a message about worth that extends far beyond the field: women can play the same game, just not with the same value.

It was a big breakthrough for women and football when I broke into the world of men's professional football as a player. However, this was not a dream I had ahead of time. I stepped up to the challenge to open that door, and I am glad I did. It was worth it because it brought the conversation about women playing football to the forefront. But, why was I the exception? Why do girls in the high school, college, and professional ranks have to be the exception on boys' and men's teams, rather than rule their own teams?

I still believe women deserve a league of their own, where they can not only survive but actually thrive financially. I love football from the bottom of my heart. I feel women absolutely have the right to play it. But what I really want is for women to have the opportunity to play this great sport against other women, in a league that is respected, supported, and properly funded. I want to see a truly professional women's football league that's as big as the men's professional league. I don't think women should have to play in the NFL to be recognized for their athleticism and to be financially rewarded for their work. Every athlete in every sport should have a league of her own, a place where her sport is on equal footing.

Why do you have to be a man to have access to the very best resources? Why can't coaching in women's football be just as desirable as coaching in the NFL? Sadly, that's not the way it works, not right now in our world, anyway. Less money is available for most female sports. The United States women's soccer and hockey teams are fighting and leading the charge despite great success and dominance in their sports. Equal pay for equal work shouldn't be so difficult to achieve and shouldn't take the threat of a boycott to get. Look at their track records. That's not fair. Tennis is probably the one sport in which women are comparably compensated, but they have still not reached parity with men.

The resources need to be put in place for women's sports to excel, and once they are, women can make a career of it. Athletes can focus on excelling at their craft, not working by day, playing by night, and fund-raising in every spare moment.

In our society, the income disparity between men and women exists in many places but few more visible than in sports. If we can fix the inequality at the bottom—where we are poorly paid and, some would argue, least appreciated, like in sports—maybe from the bottom up we can elevate ourselves to equality on other fronts. We can take one step up at a time.

The need to support women transcends sports. Women are mothers and providers and caregivers to older adults in greater numbers than men. That makes it more difficult to compete at the same level as men, to step into whatever their destiny may be, and to make a dream a reality because women have so many peripheries to focus attention on. If they're working in an office all day or pursuing their art or writing or goals on the side, it makes it challenging to rise up and get strong enough to succeed in a big and powerful way. I certainly never envisioned having to play against men to help move those chains forward.

We have to keep driving change harder and harder and making continual progress. Part of our lack of progress at equality and change is simply lack of awareness. We can't collectively or individually change something that we're unaware exists as an issue. Women's issues cannot be a quiet story that we only discuss among ourselves. Getting to the NFL—that made some noise. We need to stay noisy to create opportunities. The more breakthrough opportunities we have in unexpected places, the more places we'll make a difference, and then it is a cycle: the more the door opens, the more opportunities arise. It's called evolution for a reason. It's not like in one minute we are all of a sudden going to solve all of our inequality problems. But with continual effort in the right direction, we should start to see tiny, little cracks and then big, ground-shifting openings.

The world of sports is such a great starting point because it has visibility that other of life's arenas do not. We're drawn to sports because they champion the human spirit—the ups, the downs, the cheering, and the face painting. The heroes that emerge are universal. The sports world holds great power for improving our lives on a bigger scale. It encompasses visibility and platform. We aren't aware of a female battling it out for a top accounting job or making partner in a firm because those happen quietly and subtly in backrooms and boardrooms. But achievements in sports are done on the big screen in a big way. They are often done with public information; salaries in pro sports are made public. That's why sports are so important. Same with celebrities and politicians and public figures who have big breakthroughs. These champions are public and have endorsement deals that give them celebrity. Their struggles, therefore, represent everyone's struggles.

Take the women's national soccer team, for example. We've cheered for them and we've worn their jerseys and we've waved their flag and we've been elated with them and we've cried with them. So, we feel personally connected to them. We've seen their athletic performance, and behind that we've also seen their personal battles for equal pay for equal work. Culturally, we feel for them; as fans and their audience, we're invested. That forces all of us not only to look at that example in sports but also then to reexamine what's going on in our society and in our own lives. Are their battles our battles? And when we realize we get strength and inspiration from sports in many ways, from there, action is inevitable. We can look inward and take inspiration from those we admire. Then we use that inspiration and translate it into action.

As we expand opportunities for women, we change how women see themselves and what girls see as possible, and we change how men and boys view women and what women are capable of. We need to recalibrate how women see women and what women do for each other as well as how men see women and how boys grow up viewing girls. We need a big societal change, and the best way to do that is from the inside. The good news: it can happen. I know because I experienced it.

In the middle of my season with the Texas Revolution, my good friend Jessie Armstead of the New York Giants texted me. "Baby girl, I'm so proud of you."

"For what?"

"You're changing the way men look at women."

"What are you talking about?" I asked.

He told me that he had been at an event at Giants Stadium with some of the Giants players. They were hanging out and watching a motocross event on the big screen. One of the guys commented on how tough the competitors were and how women would not be able to tackle that particular sport because they weren't tough enough.

Another player jumped in, and what he said caught Jessie's attention. "I don't know, man. I'm beginning to think women can do anything. Did you hear about that girl playing pro football against men?" The New York Giants had noticed!

"Part of me wanted to jump up and say, 'That's my girl,'" Jessie said, "but I didn't want to taint the moment. I didn't want to change the way they were talking about you if they thought I knew you." He explained how impressed they were and how intriguing it was. Who would have thought this girl would play football against men? What was she like? How did it happen? It was all really positive. That's power. That's the power and influence that sports have on our society.

SPORT ELIMINATES OUR surface differences and teaches us that we are more alike than we are often aware, bringing us together in the process. On the teams, the novelty of my being a woman wore off within days. Then it was about my being a coach. Even in the roughest, toughest sport, these guys showed that they loved being coached by a woman. I wish that sentiment was shared in the boardroom and in the workplace and in homes and spaces everywhere. I found it in an unlikely place, but it's a lesson for all industries and sectors: if the roughest, toughest guys in sports can be coached by a woman, then there should be no limits to females in leadership roles. Men everywhere should be capable of accepting female leadership as well. The NFL was just a very visible stage.

These million-dollar players didn't simply accept a woman into their sport; they embraced me and saw the significance of it. They often remarked that this was history in the making, we were doing something that had never been done, and not just when they joked that my story would be a movie one day but also in more serious conversations. None of it was lost on them. They acknowledged the game was changing. They acknowledged the significance and helped increase the credibility of it all. I think, at times, they viewed it as a bigger deal than I did. Many of them admitted that they would get more calls asking "How is that girl doing?" than questions about their own status. It was different. No one knew what to think, and everyone had questions. Curiosity leads to innovation and change.

Sometimes I definitely underestimated the significance. For example, Coach Ross, as in Kansas City Chiefs' Ring of Honor and a great player-turned-coach Coach Ross, once commented about wanting my autograph because I was so popular. I didn't take it seriously. How could I and why would I? It couldn't be a real request. This guy didn't need anybody's autograph, let alone mine! He asked a few times and I dismissed it as his giving me a hard time.

One day, he said, "Listen, I'm starting to get offended by the fact that you will stop for everybody, you're so nice, autograph time, no problem, but I've been asking you for an autograph since we started and you have yet to do it. Take this play card and sign it for me."

I was floored. "Coach, I always thought you were kidding."

"No," he said. "In my office, back at the facility, I have a wall of honor, some of the players I've coached and others. This is history. I want your autograph to go up on the wall."

Aside from the fact that I felt horrible for not taking him seriously, I was moved that he thought of me as worthy of his wall. It struck me that if I was going to ask others to view me one way or another, I must also view myself that same way. We all must view ourselves in a positive light and be proud of what we have accomplished. Too often, many of us deny ourselves from receiving praise or embracing our bragging rights. We're too humble. We all feel insecure and get deterred by self-doubt. Girls, boys, men, and women. And to some degree, maybe that's how young girls were socialized, though I remain hopeful that's changing. But we all need to realize it's okay to be proud of our wins, however large or small they may be.

You Don't Make History by Doing What Everyone Else Has Done

The moment I made my first women's football team I promised myself I would step up to every challenge in this sport. No matter how many times I got hit, I promised to get up and do it with attitude. I committed to be every bit the professional that any professional athlete making millions of dollars would be, even though there was no money for women in football.

You don't make history by doing what everyone has done or by allowing someone else to define your worth. I found my field of dreams in the most unlikely place: on the football field. I promise you that your destiny is yours to claim as well. I want you to have the courage to change your game, whatever game you are playing. Be 100 percent authentic and always, always, always be willing to bet on yourself. Trust me, I was never the girl who was told I would make history in men's professional football three times—as a player, as a coach in the pros, and then as a coach in the NFL. At five-foot-two and 130 pounds, I was too small, I was too female, I was too everything. Have you ever been told you can't because . . . ? I was told what I couldn't, shouldn't, and wouldn't do my entire career.

The only thing I couldn't, shouldn't, and definitely wouldn't do, though, was listen to those words. I want you to do the same. Ignore the noise. Shut out the nos. Be immune to "You can't." I was called crazy by people in the business; by my family members, for giving up higher-paying opportunities; by friends, for playing football when I had so much more potential as a PhD; and by teammates, for working on my doctorate on the long bus rides to away games. But I knew every step of the way that there was more to chase, even though I couldn't quite see what it was I was chasing.

I love my brand of crazy, and I encourage you to discover, embrace, and own your brand of crazy as well. No one can see the entirety of who you are, what you are capable of, how hard you can work, and who you are destined to be. My whole life, I was underestimated and judged as too small, and yet what others saw as wrong ended up becoming what was right about me. Too small, always, but you don't have to be big to play big.

In everything you do, you have the power to exceed perceived limitations through the things in this world that cannot be measured, quantified, defined, or even explained. Live your life through the possibility of intangibles. Be the heartbeat in everything you do. Find inspiration in purpose beyond yourself as an individual. Play big.

A fierce Dallas-Houston rivalry existed for years: a personal battle between a player named Agree and me. The first time we ever met out of pads on the sidelines of an all-star game, Agree said, "Welter, how tall are you?" I said, "Five-foot-two." She said, "Shoot, you play about five-eight, five-nine."

You don't have to be big to play big.

||||||||||||||||||||||||||||||||||||||||||||||||||||||||||||||||||||||||||||||||

CONCLUSION
The Grrridiron Girl

WHEN I WAS a kid, I imagined I had wings. I believed I could do anything and be great at everything. There were no limits to my thinking. I craved greatness. I was passionate and fearless about achieving dreams.

Children are wonderful like that. Few things reflect the amazing simplicity of a quest for greatness like a child bouncing a basketball for the first time. The whole world becomes that big, round ball of possibility. The rest of the world fades away. There is no fear, no self-consciousness. The focus is the same if the child or the entire world is watching. All that matters is that ball. There is no voice of doubt, no question of possibility, no grand plan for the NBA, just the bounce.

When a child gets the feel for that ball and controlling the bounce, gradually, she elevates her eyes, and the rest of the court and the world come into view. That orange ball no longer holds every possibility. As the world comes into focus, so do possibilities and, also, limitations.

As I was taught limits, my innate curiosity, tenacious nature, and quest for greatness faded. My wings were clipped, and I started to envision ceilings and limits rather than inventions and the ability to fly. I was fortunate never to crash and burn, but I was satisfied with being great rather than pushing to be the absolute greatest.

It wasn't until I left college and looked at my safe, traditional, normal version of success that I realized I was dying a bit each day. In my soul, I knew there was a bigger destiny for me if I was willing to give up all my security, defy the odds, and bet on myself.

Finally, when I found football, I knew I was stepping into my destiny in a place that for many reasons should have been wrong. And yet, I did not become great until I embraced what made me different; my size, namely, and, eventually, being a woman actually made me special. I owned who I was and what I brought to the game, and defined my own way of playing.

Essentially, I created a superhero version of myself, the Grrridiron Girl (GG). GG was small, but her impact on the field was big. Her size and speed allowed her to elude opponents. In her chosen sport of football, getting hit was inevitable, yet this was actually one of GG's powers: when she got hit and popped right back up unaffected, she got stronger. GG had the power to change others' opinions of her through her actions, and as she acted unaffected, her force field against attack grew stronger. The stronger she acted, the stronger she became. The more powerful she appeared, the more powerful she became.

No one could hurt GG unless she let them, unless she gave her power away. GG gave her power away by letting the voices of doubt enter her mind and by letting anyone see a weakness. If she allowed the fear of weakness to enter her mind, weakness would enter her game and her physical being.

The battles GG had to win were less about her opponents and more about her inner demons, which meant she could change the game at any time.

GG had an alter ego as well, Dr. Jen Welter.

Having an alter ego is essential to maintaining a superhero self, for a number of reasons. Clearly, in the grand scheme of things, football was only a part of my life, so there had to be more to life than just the game. And having an alter ego for my super-hero self (stay with me, I promise you can use this!) illustrated that beneath the pads and the helmet, a very real, very human person exists. Perception and reality are often far apart, and though it is easy to assume that the player and the person share many of the same personality traits, this is often not the case. The very real human is different from the position the player plays on the field.

I share this snippet about my superhero self to humbly en-courage you to look at your own life and tap back into that won-derfully curious, creative child who saw no limits. The child who had wings. The child who looked at a basketball as the whole world, and literally could hold the whole world in her hands.

You have the power to create the superhero version of your-self. You just need to hold your head high and project yourself as if you have already saved the world and chosen your destiny. It's all about changing your mind-set to cut through the precon-ceived notions and the chains that are holding you back.

As you empower your inner child to come out and play for a while, I want you to tap into your very own superhero powers, not the powers you feel like you should have, but the things that make you great and that you would like to amplify so that you can put forth the best version of yourself. When you realize you have the power to establish not only your real self but also your ideal self, there is no limit to the potential. You can create scenarios for your superhero self (and alter ego) and define your actions and reactions to those scenarios. Consider it your superhero training. Couple this with visualizing your goals and destiny and you will create scenarios where your actions are so powerful, they will surprise you.

Grrridiron Girl was so conditioned to getting hit and popping right back up from years of playing women's football that when she went to the next level, and played against men, it was instinct. It was natural, and the talking smack heightened the impact. Though this was a trait of my superhero self, it was something I carried over into my real life, and you can do the same in yours.

Here's an example of how my superhero self evolved. Unlike some superheroes, Grrridiron Girl was not immortal. Though the game kept her young and young at heart, eventually Grrridiron Girl could no longer be the superhero in battle, and she had to retire her pads and helmets, but not her superpowers. She never got weaker, but her powers did evolve. She developed the ability to coach other developing superheroes to discover and embrace their own powers.

Finally, Dr. Jen Welter truly emerged and came into her own. Though Grrridiron Girl was always a part of her, she found more power in helping others embrace their superpowers than in strapping up her pads and helmet. Dr. Jen Welter had the ability to read people's eyes. She could see into their souls, see what was holding them back, sense what they needed, and coach them on how to tap into it. In growing into her new powers, Dr. Jen Welter still struggled with inner battles, and if she tried to be something she wasn't, if she lost her authenticity in any way, she lost her ability to read eyes. When that happened, she lost her ability to help and she was blinded in regard to her own gifts as well.

There is something more inside each and every one of us. Beneath the surface, the preconceived notions, the makeup, the smiles, the Instagram filters, the first impressions, and even the reflection in the mirror, who you really are, what you are capable of, the entirety of you is a perfect pool of potential. Imagine looking in the mirror and seeing not where you are currently but where you want to be. Imagine looking in the mirror and realizing you have the power to control how you see yourself and how each and every individual you encounter sees you. You have the power to use perception to create your own reality.

Know that you are a wonderful mix of everything you have learned along the way—each heartache, heartbreak, joy, fear, laugh, and tear. You have all those lessons at your disposal. Yet, no matter who you are or where you are in life, you can elevate yourself to a new version of you.

Acknowledgments

Each time you step into a new arena, it tests you, it stretches you to the core of your being, and it teaches you lessons along the way. This has certainly been the case with writing *Play Big*. At times in my life football was the easy thing, the place where I had more answers than questions. The challenge for me with this book was to translate those answers into wisdom for beyond the football field.

In collecting and sharing my life's lessons, things came full circle, extending well beyond the football field and reinforcing those very same lessons in the game of life.

Lesson one: the importance of team.

Stephanie Krikorian, my writer and so much more. Not only did I love that you literally jumped out of your seat and chased me down to say, "You have to write a book and I want to help you do it," but also I appreciate that you helped me navigate the ups and downs of the proposal process and publishing world. With each *no,* you had a *now* ready: here's what we are going to do next, even when that meant starting from scratch. Thank you for sticking with it and believing in me, and for being able to read my handwritten notes.

Maura Teitelbaum, thank you for your passionate hustle and unwavering support. You were right: it takes only one *yes*.

Thank you, Cisca Schreefel, for getting the book across the finish, and Christina Palaia, for your eye for detail.

To the entire Seal Press team: for every person who reads this book and is affected by it, I thank you for putting it into the world. It was your willingness to tell important and unique stories that brought *Play Big* together.

Lesson two: playing for something bigger, family.

There is a family of birth and a family of choice. Let's start with my family of birth, small but strong. Thank you to my mom and dad, Nancy and Peter Welter. People have often asked, "Your parents really let you do that?" That always surprised me. I was certain you wouldn't have had it any other way. Thank you for letting me live life, not live in a bubble. You have given me the freedom to fly, yet at the same time provided the much-needed security of a soft place to land in tough times. Thank you for teaching me to love fiercely and play fearlessly.

Thank you to my big sister, Rachel Welter. Words cannot express what you mean to me. You've been my best friend my whole life. I have always looked up to you, and I do not just mean those extra inches I always thought I would grow into. You're the person who always grounds me, while giving me a kick in the butt and a hug at the same time. In my most insane quests, you are a compass and an adviser.

To Esteban Martinez, my brother-in-law. Thank you for loving my sister and realizing, like I do, that she is one of the most amazing women in the world. Also, thank you for sharing your wonderful gifts with me and the Cardinals.

To my nephew, Jasper, and niece, Matto: you guys are pure joy and I love you as if you are my own, and I always will. No matter where in the world I am, you are always in my heart.

To my Aunt Jackie Welter, Ms. Lemons, it's no secret I am a chip off of your block. And I'm so glad I am. I will forever be grateful to you and Wendy for teaching me that love defies stereotypes.

To my Uncle Arthur VanLear, I would never have been able to finish my dissertation without you. Thank you for not only your quantitative analysis but also your lessons in communication and perception. Sorry, your perception lesson may not be as effective now, since the secret is out.

To my grandma and pop pop, nana and grandpa, and all the relatives who came before. I know you were among the guardian angels who have always guided me and protected me from above.

To my football family. I always wondered what it would be like to have a huge family reunion. I get it now. I found that big crazy family in football. My beautiful, wonderful football family, you taught me so many amazing things, but most importantly that diversity is strength.

To all the women in the game, thank you for always having my back while pushing me to do more and go farther; you motivate me every day. From the Mutiny and the Dragons to the Diamonds and the Energy and on to the Elite: I love you all, and I would suit up with you on any given day. And to my Team USA sisters, our bonds will never be broken. Get that gold, and never forget the pride of playing for our great country. To every player who has played and every woman yet to come, you are winning just by stepping on the field, and your worth is priceless, even when the budget is only $12.

To my NFL big brothers, thank you for all the lessons you taught me on and off the field and for how you always looked out for me, even (and especially) when I was just this crazy little female player in love with the game. Oh wait, that hasn't changed.

To the Texas Revolution organization: thank you for the wild ride and the opportunity to push past convention and change the game.

To the Texas Revs players, for those of you I had the honor of playing with and coaching. Thank you for teaching me that "the locker room handles itself" and for always having my back. And for showing everyone that just because I didn't have your *parts* didn't mean I wasn't part of the team.

To Coach Williams, thank you for allowing me to step into the men's game, step for step, and hit for hit. Playing for the team that year truly taught me how to run with the big boys. To Coach Wendell Davis, thank you for seeing something in me before I even saw it in myself and for accepting that coaching position for me even after I turned it down. You were right, not many guys were going to give me that opportunity.

To Coach Devin Wyman, thank you for all those early morning practices and, road trips, and for pushing me always, and challenging me to pick up the phone and call BA.

To BA, thank you for being the man to change the NFL for all women. I can't say thank you enough times. It took a man like you to literally bet on me and change the definition of what a coach looks like. I knew within seconds of speaking with you that I would run through a wall for you, and you definitely ran through the ultimate wall for me. Thanks for helping kick it down so I could walk through it. I am honored to call you a mentor and a friend.

To Steve Keim, thank you for bringing me into the Cardinals family and sharing all those walk-and-talk sessions in the gym, and for your continued support and friendship.

To Michael Bidwill and the entire Arizona Cardinals organization, thank you for being leaders in diversity and inclusion.

To the Arizona Cardinals players and coaches, we did the impossible and we did it well. I will forever cherish that time I shared with you. I want to thank you for welcoming me into your family. You made what could have been a difficult situation into a giant historic win, and you gave me some of the best times of my life so far. Some of the most precious moments were those in the hallways when you brought me into your worlds and into your hearts. Thank you for proving everyone wrong, embracing our differences, treating me with respect and love, and being my family. No matter where I am, I am and will always be here for you. You are all truly the HEARTBEAT of the NFL. You changed the game.

To my linebackers and our leader, Larry Foote, you have my notes, dollar bills, and a place in my heart forever. Footey, thanks for the Detroit honesty and even the farts.

To my girl Sarah Thomas, thank you for being a catalyst, a firecracker, a friend, and my sister in the Pro Football Hall of Fame. Thankfully, I never had to challenge one of your calls; however, it is epic that I can finally call a referee a friend.

To Coaches Stone, Konecki, and Mac: In 2010 when I played for Team USA, we made a promise to win gold and to become international ambassadors for the game of football. Well, we certainly won gold, and now we have continued our commitment to international expansion with our adventures in Australia. Thank you for believing in me always and supporting me in this quest. I am humbled to coach alongside you.

And to all the Australian National Team players and coaches, thank you for allowing us to be a part of this historic first women's national team.

To my dear friends, you know who you are. Whether it's been six minutes or six months, I love that we can pick up and have a great conversation like no time has passed. You know that I need you, even when I don't ask. You force me to slow down and do things that I would push past or do without (like eating or getting my hair done). You love me as much on my bad days as on my good ones, and you find my imperfections endearing. You always help me reach those things that seem beyond my limitations, including getting stuff from the top shelf at the grocery store. You force me to stop working, check on me just because, and always, always, always have my back. You keep me humble and allow me to let my guard down but also pick me up when I fall. I will work forever to do as much for you all as you have done for me. I've known some of you for a shorter time than others, but you have quickly developed equity in my life. I love you all.

To all the amazing girls and women who are playing this game, thank you, you inspire me every day. Continue to play and share your stories. In the game once known as the final frontier for women in sports, you are winning every time you step on the field. We were once the best kept secret in sports, but we are not a secret anymore.

And to my readers: Chase it down, get it done, and don't let anything get in your way. You'll get there even if you don't know exactly where it is. Thank you for reading and letting me into your world.